TO DINE WITH THE
BLAMELESS ETHIOPIANS

Kemba Saran Mazloomian

Baha'i
Publishing Trust
27 Rutland Gate, London SW7 1PD

To Dine with the Blameless Ethiopians
by Kemba Saran Mazloomian

© The Bahá'í Publishing Trust 1996
27 Rutland Gate
London SW7 1PD

British Library Cataloguing-in-Publication Data

A catalogue record for this book
is available from the British Library

ISBN 1-870989-67-8

Prolog

Dad knew my respect for the writers of antiquity. Such respect was hard to find these days, when fifteen years of living meant I'd had fifteen years to become disillusioned with the world and what it claimed to offer. But the writers of antiquity? Now they were something different; something special. Their words had continued to decorate the pages of books and the tongues of humanity: how could their greatness be denied? Though I knew nothing of Homer or Shelley or Shakespeare but that they were old, older than the yellowing paper of the old books which contained their words, I knew they'd sometimes written of truths which had not grown outdated. Shakespeare wrote of the anguish of love, Shelley of the burnout of youth, and, older than them all, Homer. Homer wrote of me. No one knew it, of course. It was a secret kept in our sunlit living room, with the rubber tree in the corner, and in the minds of the only ones who were there when the revelation was made: Dad and me.

Like I said, those were hard times. I'd grown disillusioned by a world that tried to convince me my ancestors were base, that blacks were to blame for the poverty, high crime rate and unemployment that beset them. Bitterness? I felt it every time I looked in the mirror, and saw nothing but Shame look back at me; shame to have a nose as wide and brown as a quarter pounder, shame to have hair that didn't cascade down my shoulders like the women's hair on TV. For years and years I had been sore, like a wound, and the wound seemed to be growing bigger and more painful: sore, like a wound, because the first formula I learned in school was that any word unfortunate enough to be joined to the word "black" automatically became a bad word: blackmail, black sheep, blacklist, black eye; sore, like a wound, because the first songs I learned were from taunting school friends who didn't know the harm they were doing. Songs like, "Your mama left you in the toaster too long and now you're burnt like toast," and "If you're black, step back, if you're brown, stick around, if you're white, you all right!"

But Dad knew the harm their songs caused. He also knew my secret wish to be white, to be "all right". After all, who would want to be "all wrong"? I'd mentioned this wish once, and once only, when I was four years old, when I told a neighbor I wanted to have a white mother. Would she, could she be mine? Dad saw the way I walked, with my head bent like a chicken looking for seeds, knew that I'd told my school friends to call me "Kim" instead of Kemba – my African name, which means "Faithful".

All this must surely have reminded Dad of his own anguished youth. Some time between answering phone calls for "Kim" with his firm "Nobody by that name lives here," and telling me to walk with my head held high as though I were proud to be who I was, he decided to really do something about it. This was war, between his daughter, with no respect for herself, and a whole world with no respect for his daughter, and he'd be darned if he was going to let me lose.

Oh, the tactics he used! The books he made me read, and the ones he forbade me to! The women who'd come from Detroit and Chicago, even South Carolina, bodies draped in tie-dyed African cloth and beaded braids, just to have "a little chat with the missus." The grandfather he sent me to, who rubbed my cheeks, who told me I was a beautiful black girl with skin as lovely as polished mahogany – and I had better not forget it. But disillusionment and bitterness and my soreness, like a wound, had deafened my ears to praise. Dad saw he was losing, so he changed gears. Like I said, Dad always knew my respect for the writers of antiquity, and so he used this as his final battle cry.

Sitting in the living room, Dad looked at me askance, contemplating his next move. The books he'd given me on McCoy, and on the George Washington we didn't learn about in school – George Washington Carver – had been grudgingly read, then forgotten. Those women I'd endured with gritted teeth. And my grandfather – well, he was my grandfather! Who actually believes the things grandparents say about their grandchildren? Besides, I'd heard him say the same thing to one of my cousins.

"Kemba," Dad finally said, "I've got something to show you." He sat fingering the edges of a small book while he looked out the window. What immediately interested me about this (though I tried to look unimpressed at the time) was that this was not a Bahá'í book, though so many of the Bahá'í teachings, such as the oneness and beauty of all humanity, would have been appropriate, though I thought them appropriate to my situation only in theory. Having been raised in a Bahá'í household, and now being of an age where I questioned everything about my upbringing, I allowed myself to be open only to that which came from beyond the confines of my family. I was, in a sense, a seeker, though I must have known, somewhere deep down, that my search would lead, inevitably, back to my own doorstep.

With an explosion of energy, his last all-out effort to end the cycle of self-hate the world had spun me into, Dad held up the book and said, "You see, it says here, right here, that Homer said (you do know who Homer is, don't you girl? Well anyway, he's old – old as the hills!), Homer said that the Ethiopians – the Africans! – are blameless, and that he was going to find the time to dine with them.* Then, with careful enunciation, he repeated, "To dine, Kemba. Homer said he had to make the time to dine with the blameless Ethiopians." Sinking back into the couch he breathed deeply, as though exhausted by speaking so passionately. "Yep, it says right here . . ." he mumbled, again fingering the pages of the book and looking out the window. "Now won't you believe me, girl, when I say to you that these folks who tell you that your African nose and color and hair are ugly are wrong? Dead wrong. You are beautiful because you are a child of God and because you are African. We are African, Kemba!" Dad sat up in excitement. "Look at this face. Look at

---

* Paraphrasing Homer's *Iliad*, 1:423–4: "For Zeus went to the blameless Aithiopians at the Ocean yesterday to feast, and the rest of the gods went with him."

v

me. We might have been born in America, but we are African in our features. And if white folks, and sometimes black folks too, can't see our beauty, then we have to make sure they see it. But Homer here, he saw it, Kemba! He knew the Ethiopians were beautiful and blameless. Why would he want to dine with a bunch of ugly 'blameful' folks?" Sitting on the couch on that hot, hot July day, I began to see the world – and myself – a little differently.

In the mirror I no longer saw Shame staring back at me. Now I saw a nose that was maybe just a little beautiful, and skin the color of polished mahogany. In response to friends who saw my Dad at school plays or track-meets and exclaimed, "Dang, your father sure is dark!" I no longer giggled and agreed. I would ask, "Does it bother you to see someone who looks so African?" By affirming the innocence and beauty of those ancient Ethiopians, Homer had, for me, conferred those virtues on all Africans, past and present.

And so, when the time came for me to choose where I should spend my Bahá'í youth year of service, I threw out my previous idea of going to France, and decided on Africa. Now that I was beginning to see black as beautiful, I wanted to be surrounded by a whole continent of beauty.

Learning to walk

I was living in the mining village of Selebi-Phikwe, in eastern Botswana, when I first heard the news. Another STAR ("Summer Teaching in African Regions") volunteer, named Briar, and I returned one morning from speaking to the students at a local secondary school to find a large pile of mail waiting for us on the bedroom table. Mail from overseas was rare; it intrigued us all the more since our post office box was 365 kilometers to the south. Just as we began to wonder out loud, we saw Corey's message, which he'd written on a thick package from home.

Hi Kemba and Briar! Hope everything is going well. I rode to Selebi-Phikwe on my motorcycle and obviously missed you guys, but I brought your post. Some news: there will be a teaching institute at the Bahá'í Center in Palapye. We'd like for you guys to teach a class. They'll need you back in Mochudi for the coming youth conference; cleaning, teaching around the area and letting local youth know. Oh yeah! One last bit of exciting news (as if it hasn't been so far!). Remember when I told you guys how the STAR '88 youth wanted to return to South Africa, but most of us left before we had the chance? Well, all of us – the STAR '88 and you guys, the STAR '89 – might be going there in a few weeks to help out with their first mass teaching project. Call Uncle Louie and Auntie Sylvia for more details. See ya!

*

Back home, we'd all talked about South Africa as readily as the most publicized catastrophe. Everyone that I knew was enraged by apartheid and its effects on South Africa's people. A few weeks before I was due to leave for Botswana, a girlfriend cornered me

1

in the high school hallway and warned me not to set foot inside South Africa. She'd just completed research on the country for a class project, and was fired up with righteous indignation about curfews, about "kaffir boy", about blacks getting shot in the back. This was the picture of South Africa painted for me before I left America. But curiosity often draws us toward catastrophes, and as curiosity overtook me, my fears dissolved, to be replaced by wonderment. Just a few weeks after that warning, I was there.

It's been said that the star project was initiated by a group of young Bahá'ís from the United Kingdom, as they sat round a camp fire in the middle of Botswana's Kalahari desert, thinking – dreaming – of Africa. Their inspiration was the sand beneath them, the dark open sky, the air that stirred with greetings, and, of course, the stars above. But within a few weeks, a few months at the outside, they were all bound to return home. However, the notion of "home" isn't static and unchanging. It's open to suggestion. And now these five people from so far away considered the cities, settlements, villages, deserts, deltas and cattle posts of Southern Africa "home".

Whether or not this is how the STAR project really began, I don't know for sure. The universal mind – illustrated by the theory of the "hundredth monkey" * – may have recognized the need for an organized Bahá'í youth project in Southern Africa. What I do know is, that in 1986, it officially began as an opportunity for youth around the world to serve the Bahá'í communities there; that in 1988 I heard stories of its success from a close friend who took a year off to participate; and that, in June 1989, after a training session for those about to embark on journeys to

---

* The "hundredth monkey" is a well-documented phenomenon often used as scientific proof of the existence of a "universal mind". On an isolated island, a group of scientists taught a few monkeys to wash the sand off their fruit in the ocean before eating it. The practise of washing before eating was passed from monkey to monkey. Some time later, it was noted that a group of monkeys on another island had somehow learned the same skill. The premise is that, after a certain number of minds become aware of an idea or a truth, that concept becomes universally realized.

various parts of the world, I joined a handful of young Bahá'ís in Botswana for STAR '89.

That summer there were a dozen or so youth from America, England, Zambia and Botswana who participated in the various service projects organized by the National Spiritual Assembly of the Bahá'ís of Botswana. These projects consisted of giving talks about the Bahá'í Faith at secondary schools all around Botswana, visiting isolated Bahá'ís, and assisting in the organization and presentation of youth conferences. There was also the option of travelling to neighboring countries, to assist other Bahá'í communities with their teaching efforts.

The STAR project had its own short period of orientation, during which we were introduced to local foods, languages, multi-cultural expectations, African theology, etc. Technically, the project was to last the summer (which meant the Northern summer, and didn't correspond with summer in Southern Africa: June, July and August are some of the coldest months in Botswana), but a few youth always stayed longer. Briar, Erfan and Heather left in August, leaving me the only female participant, until Helen arrived late November. There were, of course, local Bahá'í females my own age, such as Motshedi and Mel, but both of them were in school, therefore unable to participate fully in the service projects. This wasn't entirely bad; staying after the end of the summer meant that Ed, Corey and I had more time to travel to other countries.

The drive south from Botswana to Botshabelo, in South Africa, took us over hills and through valleys the color of Fall. Fifteen of us piled into Uncle Louie's truck, and we simmered in excitement for the whole journey. We were only planning to stay for one weekend in July, but plans have a way of setting their own pace. This time was no different.

The Bahá'ís of South Africa chose the township of Botshabelo as the site for their first mass teaching project for several reasons, one being its location. Botshabelo stood twenty minutes outside the city of Bloemfontein. It didn't take long for us to realize why Bloemfontein was considered one of the most segregated cities in South Africa. My first lesson in apartheid took place during our second night in South Africa, when we

3

decided to drive into town for dinner. We tried to ignore the stares from passing cars as we walked down the streets of Bloemfontein, comforting ourselves with laughter and jokes. Together, we represented the countries of South Africa, Zambia, Botswana, America, England and Iran, our skin hues ranging from deepest brown to lightest pink. We were a sight to see. Uncle Louie volunteered to be the restaurant scout, venturing inside to see if they had room for fifteen. It was Friday night and we expected the restaurants to be fairly crowded, but after an hour we began to grow suspicious.

"All these restaurants are full?" someone asked. We watched Uncle Louie as he struggled for an answer. "Uncle" Louie and his family had lived in Africa for the last twenty years. He must have known it would be difficult to find a restaurant in South Africa that allowed blacks inside, but he hadn't come out and said it. When I realized that I might not be able to eat in Bloemfontein just because of the color of my skin, I didn't know how to respond. I watched the other westerners go through interesting changes: Corey put his arm over my shoulder and announced that South African food wasn't worthy of our stomachs, and money toward it would just support apartheid. I could feel his anger heavy against my shoulders as he spoke. We found a hot dog stand that sold food to anybody, and sat down to eat on the sidewalk.

My American friends mistook my silence for pain and tried to lift my spirits by degrading South Africa. I was the only black American in our group. It seemed that my anger should have been the greatest, but rather than feel angry, I felt detached and contemplative. My only thoughts were of the stories I'd grown up hearing of my parents' childhood. My mother was the first black student to integrate an all-white high school in Orangeburg, South Carolina. The first day, the police escorted her to school, but even the government couldn't save her from the spitting and kicking and name-calling that whites subjected her to in the hallways. While the times were changing, the community didn't want to change along with them.

Then came memories of my father, raised in Detroit's Brewster Projects at a time when a police officer could shoot a

4

black man in the back for being "uppity", and not so much as an eyebrow would be raised. South Africa drew out all these memories and more, and with them I came to realize why I could feel no anger toward a country whose present mirrored my own country's recent past. Would my being angry toward South Africa for its racism be any different from feeling anger toward a toddler in its attempts to walk? America had once been unjust toward its black, Indian and Asian peoples, but was emerging into a better society; America was learning to walk. It comforted me to think that South Africa was going through the same motions. South Africa was like a beautiful lotus flower, growing out of the muddy swamps of prejudice and oppression. Some saw just the swamp and blinded themselves to the blooms, and so they left in frustration. Others saw and smelled the beautiful flower that was South Africa, and wanted to stay.

After a few days teaching in the township of Botshabelo, most of the youth had returned to Botswana with Uncle Louie. Only a few of us stayed behind, to maintain the mass teaching project in Botshabelo: Farhad, a pioneer from Iran, Erfan, and myself. Monday through Friday we'd pile into Farhad's rusty car, the back seat overflowing with copies of *The Promise of World Peace*, and sweaters that we'd shed like an extra skin as the sun chased the cold away. The Bahá'ís of South Africa invested in a hundred-man tent, which was the focal point for the teaching project. The large blue and white-striped tent stood in the backyard of a Bahá'í family's home in Botshabelo, and could be distinguished from the drab colors of the township from a mile away. A hand-painted sign on the side of the tent, visible from the road, welcomed everyone for prayers on Sunday mornings. It was then that the tent made the graceful transformation from a flag, simply signalling its presence, to a blazing beacon. The Bahá'í teachings of oneness – the oneness of God, the oneness of religion, and the oneness of humanity – have spread to nearly every country and territory in the world. These teachings were shown to be even more valid when the Bahá'ís sharing the message were seen to be as varied in religious background, country of origin, color of skin, as the world could allow. So when a community decided to focus on a partic-

5

ular area, like Botshabelo, and invite the residents for prayer and fellowship, the presence of this diversity – this living and breathing representation of what our religion stood for – was always a given.

What appeared normal to us – whether it was an English Bahá'í embracing his Sudanese father-in-law, Iranians greeting Americans, or children from Swaziland playing with friends from India – tended to amaze others. It especially amazed the residents of this all-black township in the heart of South Africa. By the second week of the project, word of our presence had spread throughout the entire township. Walking down the dirt roads of Botshabelo, people often stopped us, and, with a beckoning arm and a smile, invited us to come to their homes. They wanted to know why so many different kinds of people had come to their township to share this message. On Sunday afternoons, the Bahá'ís from surrounding countries and cities climbed back into their cars and drove home, taking with them most of the excitement and laughter. Only three of us were free from the responsibilities of jobs and family to teach full time on the project. It was a struggle to keep our spirits as high as they had soared during the weekends. We usually didn't float back down to normal until the middle of the week. It was during this time, on a cold Wednesday afternoon, that I first met Mrs Semela.

After spending a few hours inviting residents in a particular area to our Sunday prayers, Farhad, Erfan and I decided to drive to one of the schools that hadn't yet been approached by the Bahá'ís on the project. The name of the school was written in block letters near the front gate. We guessed at its possible pronunciation while parking the car. "*Mesan Youna? Mesun Yuda?* Does anyone know what in the world that says?" Erfan and I shook our heads. Farhad tried a few more times before giving up with a sigh. He tried to explain to us the importance of correct pronunciation, as if this explanation would loosen a memory that had never existed.

For Erfan and me, Botshabelo was our first major teaching project in Africa. Erfan was also a youth service corps volunteer, originally from Iran, but most recently arrived from

England. We two were giving a few months to this kind of service, but Farhad had dedicated his whole life. At the age of fifteen, he'd decided to go to another country to live, to be of service to the Bahá'í community there. Alone, he had left Iran for Johannesburg, South Africa, knowing no language other than his native Persian. His parents were, of course, sad to see him go, yet admired his willingness, at such a tender age, to trust his life to their religion, which urged its followers to spread the message of Bahá'u'lláh far and wide.

Because Farhad's experience of South Africa far outweighed ours, his suggestions and insights about how best to share the Bahá'í teachings there seemed more genuine. So the three of us stood outside the school for a good ten minutes, fumbling with the pronunciation of its name, before wandering inside. In a tiny corridor of the school's main building, a sign on a closed door read "Headmistres". Farhad knocked on the door.

"Come in please!"

A group of women were sitting around a desk, sorting papers. They looked up when the door closed behind us.

"Good afternoon," Farhad said. "How are you today?" The women stared for a moment, apparently stunned by the suggestion that the afternoon was good, then hurriedly introduced themselves. Farhad turned to us. "This is Kemba, Erfan, and my name is Farhad. We have come today with a simple request. We are all members of the Bahá'í religion, who have come to Botshabelo to tell others about the message of Bahá'u'lláh. We'd be most delighted if you'd allow us a few minutes to speak to the teachers here at . . . um . . ." – we all waited as Farhad tried to pronounce the name of the school. ". . . *Mesan Yunda?*" The women shook their heads. Farhad tried again "*Mesan Yonda?*" One of them let out a long sigh.

"*Mesan Yenda*," Mrs Semela, the headmistress, said, her chin stuck out as if she were offended. There followed a moment when no one knew what to say or do. Then she smiled. "I am pleased that you want to speak to my teachers. It is rare that we get visitors like yourselves from so far! But these are busy times – my teachers must work."

Farhad, having regained all his former confidence from Mrs

Semela's smile, tried again. "We know they must be busy this time of year, but the Bahá'í message that we are bringing is very important. We have come from all over so that it can be shared with people. Please allow us the honor to do so. If you could just spare fifteen minutes?" Mrs Semela rubbed her forehead for a few moments, flipping absentmindedly through the pile of papers on her desk. Just as I was about to accept defeat and ease over to the door, Farhad dropped the bombshell. One popular belief about foreigners, especially westerners, is that we have no respect for other cultures. If the bridge of understanding is to be crossed, it always has to be from their side to ours. That was why his words had such an impact. "It would truly be an honor to be able to share this gift with the teachers of *Mesan Yenda*."

Twenty minutes later, we stood in front of a group of thirty schoolteachers. Mrs Semela stood in the middle of the row, smiling out at us.

"So, yes –" we followed her glance as it fell on her restless teachers. "Will you please share with us this important message? We are most eager to hear."

Farhad explained that the Bahá'í Faith was a new religion that had arisen in the East. Bahá'u'lláh, the Prophet of God who founded the Bahá'í Faith, was the Promised One foretold by all the previous Prophets and in all the earlier scripture. "We believe that the Prophets of God have come with the purpose of educating mankind. Just like teachers teaching different lessons for advancing students, so the Divine Teachers such as Jesus, Muhammad and Bahá'u'lláh have come to guide mankind as we advance through different spiritual levels. Bahá'u'lláh is the latest Prophet to have come, and He has brought the teachings of oneness: the oneness of mankind, the oneness of religions, and the oneness of God."

As I handed out copies of *The Promise of World Peace*, one of the teachers asked how we wanted him to present the message to his students. Farhad's response was that he should teach them about the "three onenesses" and how small steps can help bring about peace in the world.

One of the teachers approached me while I stood arranging some Bahá'í pamphlets on a table. He asked how Bahá'ís felt about alcohol. When I said that we weren't permitted to drink, he asked, softly this time, if it would be all right if he took a few well-meaning sips every once in a while. "After all," he said, "it's not like I'm an alcoholic!"

His question caught me off guard, and I wasn't sure how to respond. How could I explain the laws of the Bahá'í Faith so that he wouldn't think that he wasn't good enough to be a Bahá'í but, at the same time, maintain the integrity of a specific religious guideline? Back home I had made the mistake of over-emphasizing the laws of the Bahá'í Faith, to such an extent that my friends had decided not to become Bahá'ís, because they believed that they first had to get rid of their little, unimportant vices. I didn't want to make that mistake again here.

I told him that Bahá'u'lláh had come for everyone, that His teachings were not meant to find us as perfect individuals, but to help transform us into better people. Attempting to live by His teachings was the best way to grow. Then, without wanting or intending to, I began talking about my father who, during the stormy discussions centered round my adolescent frustration with the world, and my rejection of religion, often compared me to the rubber tree in the corner of our living room. "If you were that rubber tree," Dad would say, "and you were given the power to draw down the shade so the light stopped coming through, would the sun care? That beam of light coming through the window is for the plant's benefit, not the sun's. You follow Bahá'u'lláh's teachings, you let in the light. You decide not to follow them, you pull down the shade." The laws of God are as binding as the laws of nature. Fighting them – which we all do from time to time – is as futile as trying to keep the sun from rising or the seasons from changing. Yet even changes in nature take place gradually. Likewise, we have to change into something better gradually.

"Yes, I understand now," he said, rubbing his chin and smiling. "The Bahá'í Faith is here to help everyone, even a some-times-drinker like myself!"

Later that day I wondered why I had referred to the advice of my father when the teacher had asked for the Bahá'í view on drinking. Throughout the conversation I'd been painfully aware of the age difference. It felt awkward, giving advice to someone who so far outstripped me in years. The only way I felt I could validate my convictions was by referring to what my father said when similar situations arose. Fathers were universally respected. A seventeen-year old held no such status. That was how I saw myself: a seventeen-year old girl traveling through Southern Africa, trying to convince others of the validity of Bahá'u'lláh's teachings. It didn't occur to me until later that anyone might see me any other way.

As we were about to leave, Mrs Semela thanked us for coming. "You have given something special to my teachers that I would never have been able to give to them." Taking my hand, she asked where we were staying.

"We don't have a place to stay in Botshabelo," Farhad said. "We've been commuting each day from Bloemfontein. But, we would love to have a place to stay here. Do you know of a place where we could stay?"

"Perhaps the girl can stay with me," Mrs Semela said, squinting her eyes and looking out the window, "but I don't know about you two. I just don't know. I'll ask around."

A few days later, I was living with Mrs Semela and her husband in the teachers' section of Botshabelo. A place was never found for Erfan and Farhad. They continued commuting from Bloemfontein. We knew, before asking, that it would be difficult to find those willing to house whites in an all-black township. Though there existed an inherent hospitality in Southern Africa, an opening up of homes and families that had all but vanished in the West, even this had its limits. Mrs Semela told me later that it was very strange to see a black girl with two white men in Botshabelo.

We sat beneath a woollen blanket, curling our toes before a heater. "Tea?" Mrs Semela asked, standing up and making her way toward the kitchen. I nodded and returned my attention to the television. The climactic scene of the evening soap opera had arrived. The young girl was returning to her room with the boy her father had forbidden her to date. The viewers knew that her father was hiding in the shadows. Mrs Semela ran back into the living room with two cups of hot tea.

10

"How can you tell what is happening, Kemba, when they are speaking Afrikaans?" She had grown weary of translating for me before the first commercial, over an hour ago.

"Soap operas are all the same," I said. Then, with a confidence that was soon to be refuted, added, "television is all the same."

The soap ended with its melodramatic conclusion, and another programme took its place. We saw a large auditorium, filled with people. A man in a light gray suit and glasses stood on stage, a group of skulls neatly arranged on a table before him. This programme was in Afrikaans too. First, the man pointed to a group of skulls distinguished from the rest by their size; they were much smaller than the others. He spoke for a long time about the small skulls, and then there were pictures of apes on the screen. We saw apes of all sizes, from all angles. It was obvious that the small skulls were ape skulls. Next, the man began talking about the larger skulls. He picked one up, circling his finger around the jaw-bone and the cheek-bone. Picking up a smaller one, he held both of them side by side for the audience's benefit, turning them sideways so that we could see their profiles. I looked at the skull closely. It was too big to be that of an ape.

I turned to Mrs Semela for explanation, but found her watching me instead, as if trying to read the thoughts forming behind my eyes. When I turned back to the television, I saw that the man and the skulls were gone. In their place were two pictures, placed side by side in the same manner as the skulls had been moments before. I recognized the picture of an ape to the left of the screen. To the right was a picture of a black man; a startled look in his eyes as if his picture had been taken without warning. I was so shocked to see a scientific documentary comparing the skulls of apes with the skulls of black people, that I sat for a few moments, saying nothing. My heart must have registered the truth before my mind did, because as I leaned toward the television screen trying to make sense of the images, my heart beat as if something wild was locked inside. Mrs Semela stood up and turned off the television.

"Kemba, Kemba, Kemba," she said to my confused frown. "They have been telling us that for so many years now; that we are from the ape and they are not." She looked out the window. "But we know this is not so. We know that we are humans just like them." We spoke for hours about those who try to convince the world that one part of the human race is lower than another. She was surprised to hear that scientists in America had at one time busied themselves with similar studies of the black population's descent from the ape. Instead of comparing skulls, they had compared the reproductive organs of apes with those of black men. The deeper the conversation dove into the issues of prejudice facing blacks on both continents, the more Mrs Semela withdrew, her comments soon reduced to an occasional "Uh-huh," her movements sharp and nervous. It was as if the same words that could heal in discussion could be turned into weapons against her.

"The Bahá'í Faith rescued me. It still does," I said, long after she had fallen silent. "When you look around you and see that everything black is equated with bad, and see your friends growing up in a world that tells them their skin is too dark, their noses too wide, a religion describing humanity as a rose garden, and black people as the pupil of the eye is a healing balm to the soul."

"For some," she whispered, "I hope it is not too late to heal." Looking at Mrs Semela's eyes, which scanned the room as if searching, I knew that she was not just speaking about those who made television documentaries. She was also thinking about her own wounds, wondering if they were too old and too deep to heal.

One of the many gifts I received from serving in Africa was the chance to discover my own sense of individual purpose and identity. Thousands of miles from home, I could no longer rely on a role developed by, and centered, around my parents. I was no longer known as Richard and June Thomas's daughter, because no one here knew them. For the first time, the opportunity was there for me to discover what it meant to be who I was, and what I could contribute to the world. My first lesson in establishing my role in a particular community, was to realize that this role had to be constantly redefined. Traveling throughout Botswana, my sense of identity focused on giving talks in the secondary schools, presenting the Bahá'í Faith to the children and their teachers.

Then I went to South Africa. I thought my old role, acknowledged and valued in Botswana, could also apply to the teaching work there. However, I was wrong. South Africa was a new stage, not only geographically but also spiritually and emotionally. I could not act as I had in Botswana, and my whole outlook had to be adjusted to fit the new community and its needs. This took time, but it was essential. My first week in South Africa was painful, as I went from feeling excited at being in such a beautiful yet tumultuous country, to frustrated, because I had to set aside the old role I was used to and discover a new one. To do otherwise would have been like trying to stuff size five feet into size four shoes.

I tried for many days to be content simply with smiling and looking "radiant" on the mass teaching trips in Botshabelo. This never gave me the same sense of satisfaction I had felt giving talks in Botswana. Part of the problem had to do with language. The official language of Botswana is English, so in Botswana I could usually understand, and be understood. The most widely spoken language in South Africa is Afrikaans, a language of German and Dutch derivation. Even though many other languages are also spoken in Botswana and South Africa, most people know the official languages, along with their own mother tongue. Nearly all the Bahá'í pioneers spoke Afrikaans fluently, and the Bahá'í teaching activities were usually conducted in that language. Sometimes a seeker would insist that they could speak English, and we'd attempt a conversation which never lasted longer than thirty seconds. My American accent was so strong that the seeker would just shake her head and ask for translation. Someone suggested that I just stand back and pray silently for the success of the other teachers, so that's what I did. It wasn't until my trip to the hospital with Mrs Semela that I began to catch a glimpse of another role I could play in South Africa.

Mrs Semela asked me to go with her to the hospital in Bloemfontein early one Tuesday morning, as I sat waiting for Erfan and Farhad to pick me up.

"Kemba, I know that you are waiting for the guys to take you door-to-door teaching, but I would be so pleased if you came with me to take my son to the hospital."

"Well, I should probably stay and help out Erfan and Farhad." I had grown accustomed to the "silent prayer" teaching method and was actually starting to enjoy it, even though I wondered if that's *all* I'd come to South Africa to do. "Yes, I really should stay." I checked my watch. In twenty minutes they'd be beeping the horn outside. I went into the kitchen to prepare breakfast. Mrs Semela followed me and sat down at the table while I sliced a loaf of bread.

"Kemba, I don't know much about the Bahá'í Faith; but, from what I do know, it is a religion that has an important message that needs to be shared with everyone." I nodded my head. She continued. "I am asking you to come with me to Bloemfontein so that you can do just that. In the city they can speak English very well and will listen to what you have to say. I know many nurses and doctors in that hospital. They need to hear the message of Bahá'u'lláh. My son, even he needs to know of these things your religion is bringing to the world. This is why I am asking you to come with me to Bloemfontein, so that you can share with people the message of Bahá'u'lláh." Pausing for a moment, she looked me straight in the eye and said, "Isn't that the reason you are here?" Rising to go, she left me standing in the kitchen, staring at the floor. "We'll leave in fifteen minutes!" she shouted from her bedroom. Half an hour later, we were in a small bus on our way to the city.

"Mrs Semela has come again to pay us a visit!" We were in a large reception room in Bloemfontein hospital. We had just dropped her nine-year old son off with a nurse who would spend the day testing him for learning disabilities.

"Yes, I have returned to see all my nurse friends, and I have brought with me this time someone very special." Putting her arms around me, Mrs Semela turned to me and whispered, "Now sing your song."

I looked at the many smiling faces, and took copies of *The Promise of World Peace* from my bag. "This is *The Promise of World Peace*." I held out the pamphlets. "A statement written

14

by the Universal House of Justice, the main governing body for the Bahá'í world community, addressed to all the peoples of the world. I have traveled from America to share this message of peace with people like yourselves." While passing out the pamphlets, I spoke about the Bahá'í Faith, and how it brings the people of the world together. I finished by asking them to carefully read *The Promise of World Peace*, and share it with their friends and families. The rest of that day, Mrs Semela and I walked around the hospital. She knew many people, and each time someone stopped to greet her, she greeted them in return by handing them a pamphlet from my bag and introducing them to me. By the end of the day, we'd mentioned the Bahá'í Faith to more people than I had smiled at in my whole first week in South Africa.

It was dark when we arrived at Mrs Semela's mother's house, just a short way from the hospital. Her mother shuffled us in from the cold and immediately called her son into the small living room to take my muddy leather shoes, to clean and polish them. "You must take care of yourself these days in this type of weather!" she fussed over me. Mrs Semela nodded and mumbled that she had been telling me to polish my shoes for days now, but, like a child, I hadn't listened.

Then something must have prodded her memory. Turning to me she said, "Kemba, where is that diary you showed me last night? I think Mama would like to hear of your last day in America."

I found my faded blue journal deep inside my bag. Sighing, I fumbled with the lock combination, opening it to one of the first entries. I felt uneasy, sharing my written thoughts and emotions with Mrs Semela, a second time, and with her mother. It was like allowing someone to see parts of me that were still developing, still tender and vulnerable. But at the same time, I could look past my discomfort and understand how important it was for others, especially those far removed from my experiences, to be able to look inside me and see that I had feelings and hopes and fears, just like they did.

The journal entry that Mrs Semela wanted me to read was especially meaningful, because it was about families and the

15

inevitable separation of parents and children. As I read aloud, the two women huddled around me as if I was a fire keeping them warm, weeping deeply and with great understanding of what it is like to say goodbye to a child. I read:

Today will be my last day in the States. Aunt Michelle came with us to the airport, looking sadly toward me and my bags piled around us. The Metro airport traffic buzzing around us prevented softly spoken words from being heard. Perhaps that's why I inched closer to my mother, trying to read from her face the words I hadn't heard when I asked her if she had any last words for her baby. Her face was at first strong and unyielding a fortress of bricks looking back at me. Then she started to tremble; the bricks crumbling and falling to the ground.

Mrs Semela's mother drew in her breath. A shudder passed through her, long and painfully felt. "Go on," Mrs Semela whispered, nudging my shoulders encouragingly. "Please go on."

When I reached out for her hand she drew back and looked away. "Mom?" I said. She bowed her head. Her baby was leaving home. I took her in my arms and spoke not a word. We sat like that for a long time a mother and daughter preparing to depart. As I held her, I felt as though I were somehow withdrawing a small portion of her strength; a strength I would need to sustain me for my journey throughout Africa.

When her shuddering stopped, I wiped away her tears and spoke the only words that I felt could rationalize the ripping away of a seventeen year old, two weeks out of high school, to a strange country so far away. "We're doing this for Bahá'u'lláh. You must remember, Mom, that we're doing this for Bahá'u'lláh."

I closed my journal and sat back. Mrs Semela and her mother sat back too, shaking their heads and weaving their fingers together. They both were crying quietly, glancing every now and then into the next room, where the children sat.

"Who is this Bahá'u'lláh?" her mother asked.

"Well, Bahá'u'lláh is the Prophet of God who founded –"

"He began the Bahá'í Faith, Mama." Smiling at her mother, Mrs Semela patted me on the knee. "I'm sorry, Kemba. Go on."

"Yes, He began the Bahá'í Faith, in 1863. As Bahá'ís, we believe that Bahá'u'lláh came to unite to the world, and His teachings reflect this: the oneness of mankind, the oneness of God, and the oneness of religion."

"The oneness of mankind?" Mrs Semela's mother asked. She turned toward her daughter.

"Yes, Mama, the oneness of mankind. That was the first Bahá'í principle I understood."

Waving her finger at me, Mrs Semela added, "I knew you Bahá'ís were different, very different, as soon as you walked into my office." Turning to her mother, she said, "They walked into my office, the three of them: a white man . . . two white men and Kemba here. Whites and blacks together sharing the same message of their religion. Ah! is that not something?"

Mrs Semela's mother stroked her chin, then asked, "So that is what is meant by the oneness of mankind; that we should see no differences?"

"That we are all one people. We are all one race, the human race, and this is most important in the end."

We were preparing to leave for Botshabelo when someone knocked on the door. One of the children answered it, and a nurse walked in. She looked at me in astonishment. "They said at the hospital that a big person has come from overseas who I must meet, but don't you look rather small!" she said.

"Oh yes," Mrs Semela said frankly, but with a smile, "Kemba is a small young lady, but she has a big message to share with people. This message is what makes her big."

The nurse had heard rumours of peace, and wanted to hear the news that she had missed. Mrs Semela gave her a pamphlet and began to tell her about this new religion whose followers had walked into her office last Wednesday morning, and whose principles would inevitably change the world into a better place.

Back in Botshabelo, I had offered to cook dinner for Mrs Semela and her husband. So I set about making a shopping list. The closest store in section H was a few houses down, Mrs

Semela told me as I headed out the door. "Just look for the peo-ple. It's in the garage of one of the houses."

The garage wasn't hard to find. Its bright aluminum door was a little more than half-way up, so most people didn't have to stoop to examine the canned goods and soda pop inside. Fresh vegetables were displayed on crates in front. I grabbed a few cans of beans, one bag of potatoes and one of onions, and placed them on the counter. "Hello, how are you?" I said to the man wearing a green plastic visor and standing behind the counter. He was scribbling on a piece of paper, and looked up suddenly, appar-ently confused, as if he hadn't heard me properly.

"Eh?"

"This is all," I said, pushing the potatoes, onions and beans closer to him.

"This is all?" he asked, nodding and smiling. "Where are you coming from now?"

"I am staying with Mrs Semela down the road."

"No, no." He waved his hands to show that he knew where Mrs Semela lived, but that wasn't the answer he was after. "Where are you coming from? Which place do you come from?"

"Oh! I'm from America," I replied.

The man began to laugh. With a scattered array of syllables, he called over the other people, who were standing in the yard looking at vegetables. They came running. "So you say," he said, speaking louder now because of his audience, "that you are from America then?" A little boy in the crowd began to talk excitedly, and was immediately hushed.

"Yes, that's right." When I opened my mouth to speak, the whole crowd leaned forward in curiosity, as if to see what it was that was making such sounds.

"Then you are a nigger!" he said to me and the crowd. "We have here a nigger from America!" he shouted, his hands raised in the air. The crowd stepped back as I pushed my way toward Mrs Semela's house, leaving a trail of "Goodbye nigger", and "see you soon hopefully, nigger", behind me, like exhaust.

I pushed my hurt deep down into the place where wounds heal, telling myself over and over again that they simply didn't know. They didn't know that the word they equated with black Americans, that they had learned from American TV and movies, wasn't our real name. How could they know that for black Americans the word "nigger" stood for slavery and lynchings and hate? I wanted to cry out, but a bitter laughter came instead. To come all this way, to a country filled with black people like myself, to find that America's racism had even penetrated Africa.

Back at Mrs Semela's house, halfway through cooking dinner, the electricity shut off for the second time. The television in the living room gave a dying whine, and Mrs Semela ran into the kitchen with a candle. "We are using too much electricity," she said, opening the lids to the pots of stew and rice, and peering inside. I tried using just one burner, but a few minutes later the power shut off again. I decided that dinner was ready. We ate silently in the dark living room. Just as were finishing, someone knocked at the door.

"This must be my friend!" Mrs Semela exclaimed. She hurried to the door. A man in a brown suit walked in. Mrs Semela, her husband, and the man began talking in Sotho. Mrs Semela spoke in a serious tone, pointing in my direction. The man spoke to me in Sotho, his face wide and expectant. I wasn't sure what to do, so I just returned his gaze, smiling uncertainly.

He cleared his throat and repeated himself. This time his brow was thick and furrowed.

"Sorry . . . I, um, I only speak English."

The man must not have believed me, because he tried again, and again, until our voices were bouncing back and forth like a rubber ball between two unyielding walls.

"Okay, okay!" Mrs Semela finally cut in, out of breath from trying to hold in the laughter which now bubbled out. "This here is Kemba – *ha, ha, ha* – from America – *hee, hee, hee* – she is staying with us for some time. And this here is my friend David from Thaba-nchu just over that way." She pointed past the hills that enclosed Botshabelo like a great hand. When she saw that David hadn't yet warmed up enough to shake my outstretched hand, she added, "And Kemba really does speak only English."

An hour later, we were talking – in English – about travel-

19

ing. "Now tell me," David asked, leaning toward me in a hushed tone as if I would divulge a great secret, "how can one, a poor man like me, have enough money to travel to the States?"

"Oh, David!" Mrs Semela sighed.

"Well, you can do what I did, and pinch your pennies."

"Pinch your pennies! Pinch your pennies! Have you ever heard anything so funny as that?" they laughed, shaking their heads at one another and pinching at invisible pennies in the air. "So then," David said, holding his stomach as if laughing had caused him pain, "you "pinched your pennies" and bought your plane ticket?"

"I worked for one summer and paid about $800 of it. My parents took care of the rest."

"I see," David said thoughtfully, and then quickly changed the subject. "Why don't you go with me to Thaba-nchu Sun?"

"Thaba-nchu Sun?" If it was anything like the Gaborone Sun in Botswana, it would be a large casino, restaurant and hotel that housed tourists from all over.

"Yes, the Thaba-nchu Sun where they have movies and shops and . . . things." He lingered on that word "things" longer than I thought necessary, and I glanced at Mrs Semela to read her reaction. She sat playing with her teacup, as if nothing strange had been said. I brushed off my concern, thinking I was just tired, and agreed to go. Since David was well into his 40s (and then some), I assumed that he wanted to show me around, in a fatherly sort of way. The wedding ring on his finger gave me further reason to believe that he would be a safe person to see the town with; especially when Mrs Semela said we'd all go together.

But after I agreed to go, the atmosphere became odd, as if a stranger had walked into the room, taking the place of the David I'd first seen in his tired brown suit. He started raising and lowering his eyebrows as he spoke to me, a crooked smile shadowing his lips. "So tell me now," he said while Mrs Semela poured us all a second cup of tea. "Do you have a boyfriend back home?" I shook my head, sure by now that my concern wasn't due to fatigue. "So you mean, if something were to happen . . . on outings such as the one we are going on tomorrow. . . anything can happen, don't you agree?"

I looked at him for a long time, before telling him that I didn't know what he meant. I was so taken aback, I didn't know how to respond. At the time I couldn't understand why a married man in early middle age would try verbally to seduce a teenager so blatantly, in front of his friends. This confusion must have registered in my expression. With an impatient sigh, and louder this time, as if my hearing had gone, he said, "What I'm saying to you is that you must agree that anything can happen on outings . . . Anything!"

Training for the Bahá'í youth service corps hadn't really prepared me for this. Nor had I had opportunity to practice assertiveness on high school suitors – there hadn't been any. But it didn't take years of dating experience to know what David was implying. I stood up and walked into the kitchen, without saying a word. I turned on the faucet, and ran the water to drown out the sounds of David leaving.

Worry about the outing had brought me to my knees in prayer, but the next day, a messenger came to the house with joyous news: David's car had broken down, and he wouldn't be going anywhere for quite some time. He sent his sincerest apologies.

Reflecting later on that evening with David, I came to understand Mrs Semela's response – or lack of it – in a new way. My own naïvety was partly because of my age. At seventeen, I was in transition, from child to adult. In many ways I still saw myself as a child, and saw my relationships with others in that light, as one young person to another or as a child to an older relative. This was the pattern I'd naturally fallen into with Mrs Semela, and – or so I thought – with her friend David. But I was becoming increasingly aware that others didn't always share my image of myself. Any image is one of many possible perspectives, and David's image of me was tainted by the portrayal of Western women in the movies and on TV, where every male-female encounter held the promise of promiscuous adventure. Whereas Mrs Semela saw an independent and self-reliant daughter, who had come halfway round the world on her own, and could surely rebuff any unwanted advances, David saw a sexual opportunity. Their responses to me, strange as they seemed at the time, simply affirmed their own assumptions about who I was.

"I am very scared, Kemba." Mrs Semela leaned wearily against her office window, watching the six students walking quickly away from us, out of the school grounds, and down the road. Though they never turned back, they must have known we'd be watching them. "I am very scared because they got your address, so that they could write to you and talk politics." Her eyes flickered like the light of a dying bulb.

"American politics?" I asked.

"No; South African politics." Sitting down, she faced me and said, "This is why those students have come here, and why they were so interested in what you had to say."

When Mrs Semela had called me to her office earlier that afternoon, threads of urgency were woven through her voice. "Come, Kemba, come, come! And bring that book of yours. There are some people here you can meet." Her office was filled with four men and two women looking awkward in her tiny chairs. "Come and tell these students about yourself. They are interested to know."

I knew then that something was wrong. Maybe it was the relief I saw in her eyes to have me center stage, instead of herself. I spoke about my country, about my life, and the reason I came to Africa. When I paused for breath, Mrs Semela asked me to talk about my plans to become a writer. I began to talk about Alice Walker, one of my favorite authors.

"This is a book by Alice Walker." I held up *The Temple Of My Familiar*, turning it over so they could see Alice Walker's picture.

"So, she is black from America," one man said.

"Yes, she is."

"Tell us now," he said, his voice concentrating on every word, "what it is like being black in America, and what it is like coming here to South Africa and seeing this country the way it is."

It was the first part of the question I heard and answered first, flipping through my past as if it were a stack of old photo albums. It wasn't until fifteen minutes later that I remembered the second part of the question, and then only because I saw Mrs

22

Semela looking uncomfortable, and wondered why.

"Now about South Africa. Your country is very beautiful. The people I've met have been most kind, but I don't like this business of the government –" my opinion on apartheid was cut short by a suddenly energetic Mrs Semela jumping up from her seat, and pushing me toward the back of the room.

"Okay!" Steering me toward an empty chair, she turned to address the students. "I think we have had a nice talk, and now it is getting late. Perhaps you should go now" she said before their protests could find voice. "Kemba, why don't you leave your address on the board so our friends can write to you."

They left as silently as they had come.

"So why did they come to see you?" I asked.

"They came to seek permission to talk to my schoolchildren about boycotting the schools of Botshabelo." Like a dream suddenly remembered, I recalled that groups of children were sitting quietly beneath the trees when they should have been in school.

"They are boycotting the schools because they are against the new government that is trying to take control here." Then her voice became small and narrow, as did her eyes. "What they are doing is not good. I refused to let them speak to my children. I called you in to show them what they should be doing. Instead of fighting the government, they should be teaching people about God's religion."

It was my last Sunday in Botshabelo with Mrs Semela, when she asked to come with me to the Bahá'í tent for prayers. "And this time I will bring my hubby, so he can see what the Bahá'í Faith is all about." When we arrived, the tent was filled with laughter. The morning prayer session was short. We sang songs, then someone gave a brief talk about the Faith. When it came time for questions, things grew silent. "No questions about the Bahá'í Faith?" the speaker repeated.

Mrs Semela rose from her seat. "I have a question about the Bahá'í Faith," she said. "I would like to know why I haven't heard of this wonderful religion before, that steers youth toward good paths and away from bad. Right now, I feel as if I

am already a Bahá'í, and have been for a very long time." At
that moment, looking up at Mrs Semela standing there before
the audience, every frustration I had felt in South Africa –
because of the barrier of language, because of my struggle to
find and understand my new role – was transformed into joy.
My purpose in coming to South Africa might not have been to
enrapture people with quotes memorized from the Bahá'í
Writings, or to speak to people's hearts in their mother tongue.
I had done neither of these things, and had previously mea-
sured my worth against those who could. But somehow, living
with Mrs Semela, I had helped her realize that the Bahá'í Faith
was something good in the world, a gift from God. Living with
Mrs Semela, I had learned the importance of constantly redis-
covering the roles we play in different communities at different
times. I had gained a deeper understanding of what it means to
belong to a family:the family of humanity where one mother's
loss is every mother's loss, and we all have to help one another
learn to walk.

*

24 August

Dear Kemba,

*As always, it was great to hear from you and follow your great
adventures as "leading lady" in the "Bahá'í in Africa" saga (smile).
Your letters have brought great joy to all of us in the community.
You cannot imagine how your experiences are affecting the spiritual
life of the community here. We look at you as our finest and best
offering to Bahá'u'lláh. In a way, you are among the first of the
youth in our community to go pioneering; and, as such, you are the
star that will guide other youth for decades to come. You probably
have no idea of the awesome spiritual ramifications of your single act
of giving up a period of your life to serve the Faith of Bahá'u'lláh.
You have earned yourself a great spiritual reward. We are all very
proud of you and the sacrifices you are making for the faith.*

  Regarding the tests you are having or were having with African men. You have been spiritually prepared to fight any and all spiritual battles that come your way. You know that tests come to us for our purification and that our only protection is prayer and obedience to the teachings of Bahá'u'lláh, and teaching, teaching, teaching and teaching. There is no other protection. Kemba, you must rise above and resist all that is counter to the glory of your great mission. Let no one cause you a second's deviation from what Bahá'u'lláh sent you to Africa to do: teach and consolidate His Faith among the Africans!

My dear Kemba, this does not mean dating or getting involved in any way with men while you are there. It means teaching and deepening them in the Faith. To do likewise is to compromise and even severely damage your spiritual credibility among the local population. They must always see you as a spiritual sister and teacher not a love-hungry American pioneer girl. Many a pioneering effort has failed this very vital spiritual test. I have no doubt that you are demonstrating to both the African believers and your fellow pioneers how a spiritually mature Bahá'í should act. Note what Bahá'u'lláh has said on the subject:

> "O Friends! Be not careless of the virtues with which ye have been endowed. Neither be neglectful of your high destiny. Suffer not your labors to be wasted through the vain imaginations which certain hearts have devised. Ye are the stars of the heavens of understanding, the breeze that stirreth at the break of day, the soft-flowing waters upon which must depend the very life of all men, the letters inscribed upon His sacred scroll."

You must write your old high school friends, Kemba! They have been running to the mailbox all summer long looking for a letter from you. But remember, honey, letters can either help or hinder the soul! Try not to write "old world" letters about cute boys. Remember, you are a spiritual star! Guide your friends in your letters as did Martha Root and Dorothy Baker. Uplift their spirits. Teach the faith in your letters. Deepen your Bahá'ís friends here at

25

home in your letters. Be all that God created you to be: an eagle! I love you, Kemba, so very much. You have made my life worthwhile. I could leave this plane of existence fully satisfied that I fulfilled my obligation to God, to bring forth someone who will make mention of God!

Dad

Pecan pie and parliament

The second time I saw Jane was on a warm November afternoon. The Gaborone mall was filled with marching, singing schoolchildren promoting a school play, with men behind their handicraft stalls, and hundreds of other faces which merged into one anonymous wave ebbing and flowing along the walkway. Crowds could be like that, moving harmoniously, by force of communal habit. A foreigner in such a crowd could be as obvious as the sound of a flute when the score calls for trombones: not discordant enough to make you wince, but still too loud to ignore. That was how Jane appeared that day, walking too slowly past the malachite statues, spinning round too quickly to see if the man laughing behind her had noticed the tiny bald spot in her hair, and calling out too loudly when she saw me across the square.

"Kemba? Oh good, it is you. What's been up?"

"Nothing much. How've you been?" At first I couldn't put a name to the face, or recall where we'd met. I stalled for time. "So . . . haven't seen you in a while. Where've you been?"

"Oh, you know." She looked back at the rows of leather sandals, then took a quick glance at her own worn down shoes. "I've been here and there. Still missing home though, you know?"

"Yeah, I sure do." That had been the clue I was waiting for. It wasn't until then that I noticed her American accent. She had been with a group of Americans at the Gaborone Fair, and that was where we'd first met.

That second day of the fair, a group of sunburned Americans wandered into the Bahá'í booth, and warily looked around. I watched them from a little distance for a few moments before approaching them. They must have recognized my smile as a

27

prelude to religious proclamation. Before I could utter a word, they'd dispersed to the corners of the booth. All, that is, except Jane. Her feet stayed firmly in place, and when I offered her a smile, she gave one in return. Assuming she was from Botswana, because she stayed to greet me, I addressed her as I everyone else I'd spoken to at this event.

"Hello! Welcome to the Bahá'í booth. Would you like to hear about the Bahá'í Faith?"

It had taken me several weeks to feel comfortable with declaring my intentions so straightforwardly. I had grown up believing that teaching the Faith demanded caution above all. Though such an approach was often necessary if American Bahá'ís were to reach beyond the fears, superstitions, and traditions of their fellow citizens, it wasn't necessarily appropriate for teaching the Bahá'í Faith in other cultures. In Botswana, people were not afraid to openly discuss their religious persuasion – or any other type of persuasion for that matter. There was no need to beat about the bush, you simply had to dive in.

I had become so accustomed to the open and frank curiosity of Batswana * that I didn't recognize Jane's American circumspection.

"No, I'd rather not hear about your religion, if you don't mind," she said. "I've got one of my own."

I was so surprised, I didn't know what to say! Not interested in hearing about a new religion? I hadn't been given a line like that since leaving the States. I managed to mutter an unconvincing, "Oh, okay. That's fine. Would you like to look around?"

Jane nodded, and began to walk the length and breadth of the booth. "You're American," she said over her shoulder. "Which part do you call home?" Then it all began to make sense; she was American, not Motswana. I mentally shifted gears. We began a conversation which was framed by our mutual joy at being somewhere where our skin color no longer made us feel odd. Reverting to the standard American approach, I mentioned the Bahá'í Faith covertly, dancing around the edges

* The plural of "Motswana", a citizen of Botswana.

of the principles and teachings, so that in the end she asked me, "Now what's this Bahá'í thing you keep on not mentioning?"

"Well, I don't have long," Jane said, digging deep into her bag and pulling out a creased sheet of paper. "I just wanted to invite you to a black American Thanksgiving celebration. Some of the black Peace Corps volunteers, like myself, and other black Americans will be there." In my hand she left the map showing where the event was to be held. The date of the celebration was the same day that Helen, an Ethiopian-American Bahá'í youth volunteer, was scheduled to arrive in Botswana. Because I knew that Helen was flying that day and would miss her Thanksgiving meal, and because I'd always wanted to meet the black Americans in Botswana, I happily accepted Jane's invitation; asking in jest if there would be any sweet potato pie – a soul food delicacy I adored – and settling instead for her assurance of pecan.

Thanksgiving morning I went to the airport with Mel, daughter of Uncle Louie and Auntie Sylvia, to await Helen's plane. When it was announced that the plane would be delayed, leaving us nothing to do but watch the airport officials fuss over the weight of luggage, I filled time by telling Mel about Jane, and the invitation to the Thanksgiving celebration later that day.

"So: this is for black Americans?" Mel asked when I'd finished. I nodded. "Oh. I see."

The intercom announced the arrival of Helen's plane. We ran to the windows to watch the plane touch down and release its stream of weary travelers. With her face to the glass, Mel said, "So, you're taking Helen, and who else? I stared at her, confused. "What do you mean, who else? I only know of two black Americans here: Helen and me." The passengers from the plane reduced to a trickle. Helen limped out of the plane, her knees stiff from the journey, and Mel and I forced bright smiles for her arrival. On the drive home, our conversation held no evidence of the underlying tension that was growing because of the Thanksgiving celebration. Instead, it lay carefully concealed beneath our jokes at the expense of the cows, standing like statues in the middle of the road, and other such sights. The celebration was not mentioned again until later that afternoon. It re-emerged, at first, as a joke. How was I going to get to my blacks-only Thanksgiving celebration, Mel wanted to know. I told her that the car-less guests were going to be picked up at Independence Avenue at ten minutes to five. Rather than satisfy her curiosity, my explanation served as a catalyst for the release of anger from her, and marked the beginning of a painful process of self-evaluation and change for me.

Mel wanted to join us at the celebration and could not understand my hesitation to have her come with us; a hesitation which later turned into outright refusal. Though Mel had been born and raised in Botswana, she held the American citizenship of her parents and considered herself an American. She also wanted to meet the black Americans living in Botswana. Why should she be denied this just because she was born with white skin? I passionately defended my right to gather exclusively with black Americans. Mel knew I wasn't racially prejudiced! Besides, the invitation was specifically for black Americans only. How could I be expected to go against my hostess's request by bringing someone who obviously wasn't invited?

Yet, on the inside, I wavered with doubt. Wasn't I a Bahá'í, a member of the only religion to teach that everyone should be looked upon as members of one human race? Wasn't uniting the world and its diverse peoples all about bringing them together, not continuing to push them apart? Would I be going against everything I *thought* I believed and stood for by refusing to bring Mel along, now that she'd asked to come?

The debate raged inside me, long after Helen had taken me aside and quietly explained that Thanksgiving held no meaning to her. After all, she was born in Ethiopia, and had been raised there, and in Germany. The States just happened to be her present home. When bitterness drove us to attempt a resolution, Mel explained her hurt, anger, and confusion that I would even consider attending a social event solely for black Americans. She would never have considered going to a party to which only whites were invited.

I tried, but I could not shape my feelings into words. How could I explain my many-sided personality, convening like a

30

parliament inside my head? How could I explain the voices that vied for attention, for preference and power? My black voice longed for the comfort of sameness and acceptance that the Thanksgiving celebration offered. In a room of others who shared my color, my features, my language – and my background of American racism, I could feel as though I belonged. Just when I was tempted to listen to this voice which had, for far too long, been shushed and ignored, another voice shouted out its views. What about the Bahá'ís? What about the members of my Bahá'í community back home who were struggling, as I was here, to accept all cultures and colors? What about America's racial conflict, which Shoghi Effendi had told us was "the most challenging issue?" What about the light of unity? What about seeing the end in the beginning; my action as a small step in the elimination of prejudice? Okay, what about this:how is my excluding Mel from the celebration because she has white skin any different from all the things my parents, and their parents before them, were excluded from because of their black skin?

Then an impartial, nostalgic voice, which should not have been involved in the first place, reminded me of something I had nearly forgotten. I had been twelve years old and tired of feeling along in my blackness at middle school. It hadn't been about having friends; I had plenty, of all colors and nationalities, even one who was black like me. But it had not been enough. I wanted more. I wanted to be surrounded by dozens – hundreds – of black friends, if only to confirm my normality. The closest school fitting this requirement was Hannah Middle School a few miles away, in a different school district. My parents approved the switch, and at the start of my final middle school year I began as a student at Hannah.

I was guiltlessly enjoying myself and my new friends until a neighbor's son noticed my absence from the old school bus. One day our neighbor was trimming her hedges, and my dad was trimming ours, when the inevitable question arose: where has Kemba gone? Dad told her that I wanted to be around more black kids, so I had changed to another school. Dad's impersonation of our neighbor's startled "Oh!" made me think about who had actually benefited from my actions. So I was now comfortably surrounded by others who looked like me, but had my actions brought anyone one step closer to solving the problem of racism? What did my personal comfort mean to our neighbor's son or to the other members of my old, nearly all-white school? Perhaps we all could have learned something from my discomfort had I stayed. The other students could have learned that the world comes in shades other than white, and I could have learned that it was often uncomfortable to be a part of a society still in the early stages of coming to terms with its diversity, that growth and awareness cannot come about without that very discomfort.

Though it was this final, nostalgic voice that waxed strongest for me, I did not feel ready to handle the rejection I feared I'd receive if I showed up at the Thanksgiving celebration with Mel. So in the end I decided not to go, insisting that I no longer wanted to, which, in a way, was true. But the discussion with Mel – and with the parliament inside my head – had not been in vain. I went to bed that night with one realization: if we Bahá'ís really do want to be members of a united, diverse and multi-faceted community, then we are in for a lot of hard work and discomfort along the way.

Mosi Oa Tunya:
"Smoke That Thunders"

An old train with only three passenger cars carried us from the capital city of Namibia to the outer edge of Botswana. I was returning from a teaching trip in Northern Namibia, along with Corey and Ed (two American Youth Service volunteers). We were heading toward a few isolated villages in Botswana to conduct delegate elections. Ed and I were going to hitch-hike to Ghanzi, Maun, Nata and Kasane. These were the most accessible villages we had been asked to visit by the National Spiritual Assembly of the Bahá'ís of Botswana. The three of us had spent hours studying the map, so we knew that these villages formed a triangle – Kasane to the north, Nata east and Ghanzi west – and we knew, almost by heart, which routes from village to village were paved, unpaved, or didn't exist at all.

Corey had been assigned the most remote villages to contact for delegate elections. These villages were tucked within the Kalahari desert, which stretches across most of Botswana, so they could only be reached by vehicle. After reaching Ghanzi, Corey would hitch-hike south-east toward the capital city, Gaborone. From there, some self-sacrificing Bahá'í pioneer would hand over the keys to his 4x4, and, stocked with Bahá'í books, Corey and a young African Bahá'í named Elliot would drive into the desert, in search of the Bahá'ís who lived there.

At Sandfontein, the border control post on the Namibian side of the border, we waited hours for a ride to Ghanzi. Drivers passing through the border had offered to take one of us, at most two, but we had declined. We wanted to stay together at all costs, at least until we got to Ghanzi, where we would go our separate ways.

By midday, the traffic through the border had thinned to one vehicle every hour or so. We knew it was unlikely that we'd find rides for the three of us that day, but we decided that at least one should get to Ghanzi that evening. The next time someone offered one of us a ride, Corey went ahead, leaving Ed and me playing idly with flattened pop cans. No one crossed the border again until a few minutes before five. After the red 4x4 pulled up to the passport and custom control office, a border guard ran to the gate and locked it shut. It would stay shut till eight the next morning. I began to feel uneasy as I realized two things: we might have to camp out at the border and we hadn't brought tents to sleep in, and the licence plate on the 4x4, our last hope to cross the border that day, was South African.

Ed stood up, brushing the sand off his pants. "Okay kid, wish me luck or something," he mumbled, then ran after the man who just stepped out of the 4x4. The man stopped reluctantly, frowning. Ed tried to win his sympathies, holding his hands together as if praying and bowing slightly.

"Oh, alright," I heard the man grumble as he walked toward the passport office. Ed gave a victorious grin and a raised fist salute. We'd gotten the lift.

"But I'm warning you," he said before locking us into the back storage area of his 4x4. "It's going to be a bumpy ride. I've got to drive fast over the sand or I'll get stuck." When he said a bumpy ride, I expected something that could at least be slept through. What I hadn't expected was a four-hour drive over sand so thick that the whole truck bounced up and down. The passengers in the front were held down by seat belts, but there were no belts in the back, and we bounced off the metal walls and roof like dice in a gambler's hand. For the first hour, we tried to carry on a conversation, to take our minds off our circumstances. This lasted only until we went over a large sand dune and our foreheads knocked, causing both of us to cry out. I was happy when darkness came, and Ed could no longer see the tears staining my dusty face.

We had agreed to meet Corey at the hotel in Ghanzi that night, if we ever made it off the border. There was only one hotel in the village. The driver of the 4x4 helped us pull our bags out of the back, pointed toward the hotel through the dark, and drove off. We couldn't see it, but we could hear the music and laughter swaying in the air like a banner. Halfway to the hotel, I stopped and put my bags down.

"Ed, I think something's missing."

"What?"

"I think I left a bag in the truck." We felt through my bags in the dark. I had left my sleeping bag in the 4x4. We walked toward the hotel in silence. A sleeping bag is essential for a hitch-hiker traveling through lands unknown. Without that vital piece of vinyl and cotton, there's no comfortable way to sleep unless every night is spent in a hotel. Without a sleeping bag there was no protection from the hot sun and stinging sand while riding in open-backed trucks, and no padding against bumpy rides. My only consolation was the knowledge that the night would be spent in a soft bed at the Ghanzi Hotel – or so I thought. We flipped through the guest book at the front desk, until we found Corey's name. The first thing that caught my eye were the words Corey had written beneath the room number column: "camping out". I gasped. Ed looked at me and shook his head, writing his name inside the guest book and including those same two words: "camping out."

"I'm getting a room, Ed. I don't care what you and Corey do. I have to get a room!" I couldn't imagine camping out without a tent or a sleeping bag. The desert temperature might reach over a hundred during the day, but at night the air grew so cold it put frost on the grass, especially in October.

"Kemba," Ed said, looking at me with an air of rationality that I found slightly disturbing. "A room costs 61 rand." Then he sighed heavily, as if explaining something to a small child. "You can't afford it, and neither can I. You remember how much money our plane tickets to Windhoek cost?" I nodded; an unexpected journey by air had cost 290 rand. A few weeks ago Ed, Corey and I had made plans to take a bus to Windhoek, capital of Namibia, to assist the Bahá'í community in a teaching project they were facilitating in a village named Rundu on the Namibian/Angolan border. As were boarding, we found out that the fare could only be paid in cash, not in travelers' checks as we had assumed. Since none of us were old enough to rent a car, our options were limited to the train at 239 rand, and an economy class flight at 290 rand. Price would have been the deciding factor if it hadn't been for the time. The Bahá'í caravan was leaving Windhoek for Northern Namibia in two days. The train took three days to travel the 1800 kilometers from Johannesburg, to Windhoek while the plane only took a few hours. Our decision to fly set us all back financially and we had to spend the next few months cutting costs to make up for it. But did that mean we had to jeopardize my health now?

"Remember Ed, I don't have a sleeping bag," I said through clenched teeth.

"We'll figure something out." Twenty minutes later, I sat watching our bags beneath a small picnic shelter. I could see Corey and Ed sitting at a table outside the restaurant, their heads bobbing over their plates as they ate. When they finished their steak and chips, it was my turn to eat. I found a seat at the same table, but a sleepy-eyed waiter told me that the restaurant was now closed for the evening. If I wanted peanuts and soda pop, I might try the bar out front. I ventured only a few steps into the bar, which was dimly lit and filled with leering men. I decided that food could wait until morning. By the time I got back to our camping site, Ed and Corey were fast asleep in their sleeping bags, and I was furious.

The earth was warmer than the concrete picnic table, so I spread my thick bush skirt and a few clothes over the grass to make a bed. I laid down, but not before giving Corey and Ed spiteful glances for their thoughtlessness.

"Whatever happened to chivalry?" I asked their snoring figures. "And what else in the world could possibly go wrong?" I should have known better. My answer came as a grumbling in the western sky which drowned out the music from the hotel. Then the sky opened up and rain fell.

I awoke the next morning, feeling strengthened by the trials of the previous night. I'd survived a cold night of hungry mosquitoes, loud music and rain, all without a sleeping bag or a tent. With those achievements under my belt, I felt ready to handle the task of delegate elections. Ed and Corey were still asleep when I walked through the back entrance of the hotel to the bathroom. I didn't notice five pairs of eyes watching me from behind a trash heap until I was a few feet away. The dogs jumped out, barking and growling, ears pressed back against their heads. "Get back!" I roared. Almost in mid-leap, they circled back to their hiding places in the trash, tails between their legs. I didn't realize how instinctively I had warded them off until minutes later, washing my face in the bathroom. I thought about other times I'd been threatened by angry dogs; never before had I been able to shout them into submission.

As I walked back to the campsite, I saw Corey coming from the hotel, a green package in his hands, whistling to himself. As he passed by the lair of the angry dogs, they leaped out, barking furiously. Corey stopped in his tracks, swivelled around, and ran from them. The dogs didn't stop chasing him until he was around the bend and out of sight. I was still laughing when Corey appeared again, having found an alternative route to the campsite.

"Look what I found!" he shouted. "Someone left your sleeping bag at lobby desk. It's a good thing I went in there to check on it for you, or you'd be doing all but whistling Dixie!"

Ed was still asleep when I walked Corey to the edge of town later that morning. A white gravel road led past clothing and food stores, to a section of town where there was nothing but empty desert to either side of us. Even the few rondavaals * on the outskirts of town seemed swallowed up in the desolation. I left Corey sitting at a mud-walled shelter by the side of the road, built for people waiting for a lift out of Ghanzi. It was cool and dry inside, and you could see cars coming from a long way in any direction. When Ed and I went back to check on him late that same afternoon, there was a group of boys with chickens dancing barefoot on the floor of the shelter. Corey was sitting on a ledge gazing blankly down the road toward Ghanzi.

"Oh, I don't know what they're doing here," he said wearily when we asked about the children. "They just came all of a

---

* Round clay dwellings found primarily in the villages and smaller towns of Botswana.

sudden, fooling around and chasing chickens. Just a little bunch of nippers." Dragging his eyes from the road, Corey smiled at the children. They had stopped their dancing and now stood watching us in amazement. "Was it something we said?" Ed asked. The children looked at one another, giggling. Then they began to shower us with "hello" and "see-ya" and other scraps of English they'd collected in their seven or eight years.

When we went to check on Corey again the next day, he was gone; nothing left of him – or the chickens – at the tiny shelter except a handful of feathers and a scrap of cardboard on which was written in big bold letters: GABORONE.

While we were in Windhoek, a young Scots pioneer by the name of Alan gave us photos of a few of the Bahá'ís in Ghanzi. Alan had taken the pictures a few years before when he was at the village as a youth volunteer in the same STAR project in which Ed, Corey and I were currently taking part. I didn't know at the time how important the pictures would be in helping us find the Bahá'ís. The National Teaching Committee of Botswana had prepared an elaborate delegate election kit for each village in Botswana with Bahá'ís. The kit included a list of all the Bahá'ís, their post office box numbers, and their occupations. There are usually no addresses or street signs in villages with rondavaals or houses haphazardly placed. Most people had a box number at the local post office, which was how they received their mail. Their occupations, we eventually discovered, was one of the few ways to find Bahá'ís in towns that sometimes had populations of up to 50,000. While some occupations were as vague as "field worker", and "store clerk", other occupations were more revealing: teacher, student, doctor. In these cases we went straight to the local schools or hospital, asking around for that particular person by name.

Also included in the kit were typed letters in Setswana, the language of Botswana, and election ballot papers. The letters were addressed to each Bahá'í's post office box number, telling them that it was time to elect delegates, what electing delegates was all about, and a blank section where Ed and I were to write in the place, time, and date of the elections. The directions in Setswana told each person to vote for one Bahá'í whom they felt was best suited to elect members of their National Spiritual Assembly in the National Convention a few months later at Mahalapye. All this information was stamped and addressed so we could send them off to the Bahá'ís if we were unable to locate them personally.

That first morning in Ghanzi, after checking our bags behind the front counter of the hotel, we began our search for the Bahá'ís. Our first priority was to find a man called Bridge. According to Alan, Bridge lived in a large house and was always more than happy to allow Bahá'ís passing through to stay with him. Until we found him, we would have to stay in the camping grounds.

In Botswana, like most other countries in Southern African, people make great efforts to ensure that all the members of society are taken care of – a form of "social security" that isn't funded by the government. In its most general sense, it works like this: if one person has something that can be of benefit to another, it is their social duty to share it. One of the pioneers in Botswana recounted a funny story about how they came to realize the importance of this system. When they first arrived in Botswana from America, they had a sizeable sum of money which they invested in a house and a brand new land rover. A few days after the papers had been signed and finalized, they heard a knock at the door. They answered it, and there stood a young woman who said she'd come to do the cleaning. The pioneers told her she'd come to the wrong address. But the next day another young women came to the door, stating she'd come to prepare their meals. Thinking that some disorganized maid agency must have been confusing them with someone else, they asked their neighbors' advice on rectifying the situation. That's when they were told that "help" would come every day until they decided on someone to do their general housework and cooking. They were told that, while hiring household help in America was considered snobbish and only for the well-off, in Botswana it was expected that those with larger incomes would distribute their wealth to other members of the community by hiring people to take on household duties.

39

This system also worked for transport and shelter. There were informal "hitch-hiking posts" all over Botswana, where people would wait for lifts. Rarely would drivers with seats to spare drive past without stopping to inquire who was going where, and offer a lift to as many as they could safely accommodate. People were equally as generous with a spare bedroom or empty floor space. While in America we would never hitch-hike, or ask a stranger if they knew of a place to stay, this was an acceptable part of Botswana's culture, without which we would never have got very far outside Gaborone. We were, of course, careful not to take this generosity for granted, returning the favor through petrol money or groceries, or at the very least a word of thanks.

The Ghanzi hotel was eerily quiet compared to the night before. The only person in the lobby was a young woman sweeping beer cans into a pile.

"Excuse me, Mma. We are Bahá'ís looking for Bridge." I showed her the picture of a smiling man standing in front of a pale green house.

"Yes, I know Bridge." Leaning against her broom, she scrutinized the photo, then looked curiously at Alan's other pictures, which she saw in my pouch. I took them out, and let her see them: a group of youth in front of a disheveled land cruiser, a large man posing stiffly with Alan. "Yes, that's Computer – and I know him too," she said, pointing to the large man. She didn't recognize the girl in the last of the photos. The name on the back was Jacqueline.

"I'll take you to find them just now." Taking the broom, she went through a door marked "private" and returned with a large black umbrella.

"Will you tell me about the Bahá'í church?" she asked as we walked down an empty road with no shade except for the umbrella she held over our heads. She interrupted us only once, to throw what sounded like an insult at a passing man. "He's a Bushman," she told us. Ed and I looked at her, then at each other. We couldn't see how he was any different from her: both had the same narrow eyes and caramel-colored skin.

I had been told before that the Bushmen were at the bottom of the social ladder in Botswana. Their situation was comparable to that of the Native Americans; both were among the first to live on the land, and were among the first to be expelled from the land when its value was realized. They were often reduced to living in remote, barren areas of the Kalahari. A few weeks earlier I had made a connection between the two that went beyond a mere intellectual understanding. I was one among a group of fifteen Bahá'í youth that took a trip deep into the desert. We were to visit the Basarwa tribe who lived in a tiny settlement that appeared to rise out of the sand as we approached it. That evening, they sang for us. Closing my eyes, I could have been at a Native American powwow back home in Michigan.

The woman from the hotel lobby led us to the secondary school, where hundreds of people stood in lines, holding umbrellas for shade. She told us that the whole town was here, waiting to vote in Botswana's national elections. She disappeared into the crowd and returned with a broad-shouldered man, who introduced himself as "Computer". Squinting at the picture I held out for him to see, he smiled and asked about Alan.

"Alan's doing well," I answered, thinking back to the first time I'd met him, at a Bahá'í wedding in Windhoek. Two features immediately betrayed Alan as a foreigner to Namibia's heat: his sunburnt face and leather pants. Later I learned that he was a pioneer from Scotland, who'd brought with him a refreshing honesty, balanced with humour and charm, making him an excellent story-teller and adviser. It was difficult to forget Alan once you'd met him, so I wasn't surprised to hear him so well remembered in Ghanzi.

"Alan's doing just fine. But he did seem to miss Botswana. He spoke often of his love for Botswana, and how he missed the closeness of the Bahá'í community in this country."

"Yes, I can see why that might be so," Computer said. "Namibia, where Alan is now living, is a country of cities, where people don't have enough time. But Botswana is a country of villages. Here, we always have time. Time for friends and

41

family, time for leisure, time to stand in queues all day and vote . . ." Turning toward the crowd, he added, "You do know that this is time for elections?"

"Yes, we do know," Ed said. "Kemba and I have come for another type of elections: Bahá'í elections. We've been trying to locate the Bahá'ís and get them together to vote. But in the meantime, we really need a place to stay."

"This is the time for national elections!" Computer repeated. "It will be very hard to get the Bahá'ís together. You should find Bridge. He will have a place for you. I must get back before I lose my place in the queue."

We found Bridge playing darts in the hotel bar. Our escort stood watching him with her hands on her hips for a few moments before shouting out, "Bridge, these people have been looking for you all over town; they are Bahá'ís from America."

It didn't take long for Bridge to gather together four local Bahá'ís in the hotel lobby. Everyone promised to come to a meeting we set up for nine the next morning and to spread the word around to the other Bahá'ís. Afterwards, Bridge took us to his house and showed us a small room with a table and three chairs.

"You can stay here," he said. Ed and I happily consented. We had a roof over our heads, and walls to protect us from the rain and mosquitoes. After the previous night I'd learned to count my blessings, however small my Western mind made them out to be. The next morning we got up early to prepare the room for the meeting. Waiting for the Bahá'ís to arrive, Ed and I had joked about the advice we'd received from friends in Gaborone, that we go ahead with delegate elections no matter how many we could round up, even if it was only one person. But we thought we had the situation under control. Two hours later, we were still waiting. None of the Bahá'ís had shown up for the meeting. It was well past noon when Bridge burst into the room, a surprised look on his face at seeing just Ed and me.

"Let's get Computer," Bridge suggested. "He can take us in his car to find the Bahá'ís. It will be easier that way. The sand on which Ghanzi was built rose to our calves as we trekked through it, our arms swinging like pendulums as we fought for strength. Computer wasn't at his house, with its trimmed lemon tree in the front yard, nor was he at his mother's. So on we went, tongues dry from the heat, to a store to buy drinks. The store was a large house with a wide porch painted bright blue. Even from a distance, we could hear the shouting and see fists raised in celebration. I bought us all Cokes, and we sat on the porch in the center of all the excitement. Everyone was happy about the election results. The news had come that morning that the Democratic Party, the ruling party for the last 23 years, had won in the Ghanzi district of Botswana. "I'm just a civil servant," Bridge answered when I asked if he was glad they had won.

We weren't able to hold our election until late that evening. We guessed by the absence of the other Bahá'ís that the village-wide celebrations were much more exciting than electing Bahá'í delegates. The only Bahá'ís we were able to gather up were Bridge and one of the men living with him. Even that late in the evening, the celebration was still going on. Trucks filled with shouting people drove down the road in front of Bridge's house as we said prayers and presented the two with copies of *The Light of Bahá'u'lláh* written in Setswana. When it came time for them to vote for a delegate, they cast tied votes three times in a row, until Ed explained that if they kept voting for them-selves we'd be there all night. "What do we really believe as Bahá'ís?" Bridge asked when the voting was over and we sat absorbing the energy from outside.

"Well," Ed began, "as Bahá'ís we believe that no man or woman is better than any other man or woman. We believe that all of humanity was created from the same dust. This means that you are no better than me because you have black skin, and I am no better than you because I have white skin. One of our goals as Bahá'ís is to try to obey all laws laid down for us by Bahá'u'lláh." Bridge nodded his head as Ed spoke, rubbing his knuckles and thinking. "Yes, it is important that we obey these laws of Bahá'u'lláh, so people know that we are serious when we say that we are Bahá'ís. So that people know that we are Bahá'ís on the inside, and not just on the outside."

We sat and watched the trucks filled with exuberant people drive past. Their headlights spotted the trees like flashes of lightning. By midnight, fireworks were popping in the sky.

*

The population chart showed Maun to have anywhere between 5,000 and 50,000 people. This settlement was on the south-eastern edge of the Okavango Delta, a swamp rich in plant and animal life that brought tourists from all around the world. Though Maun sat near the richest water supply in Botswana, it was a dry, dusty place. The only sign of the swamp lands close by were the curio shops, the travel agencies along the side of the road, and glimpses every now and then of a river in the distance. Ed and I spent the morning of our second day in Maun walking along the main two-lane road in search of the Bahá'ís. All we had was an alphabetized list of names, occupations, and birthdays, and a picture of a girl named Jacqueline. Bridge sighed happily when we showed her picture to him in Ghanzi.

"Isn't she pretty?" he had asked Ed. Ed nodded. We assumed that Jacqueline was Bridge's girlfriend, and even if she hadn't been so beautiful, we weren't about to insult the girlfriend of the man who had housed us for four nights!

"Yes, she's awfully pretty," Ed added. Even Alan hadn't been able to resist, commenting on her beautiful smile, when he had given us Jacqueline's picture.

"Yes, she is. And you better not touch her," Bridge told Ed with a sly smile. "Do you know why?" Ed shook his head. "Because she's my sister."

In Maun, we stopped at many of the shops near the road, where women working behind the counters gathered around our list of names, shaking their heads. They knew none of these people. For lack of a better plan, we decided to follow the main road winding through Maun. As we walked, the road gradually became crowded with uniformed schoolchildren walking in the same direction as we were. When the road forked, we followed the children along a trail to the right. Soon we could see a secondary school in the distance. "Why don't we try and speak at the schools in Maun while we're looking for Bahá'ís," Ed suggested. "Maybe we'll find Jacqueline at one of them." Bridge had told us that she went to boarding school in Maun. We weren't sure if this was the right school. We showed her picture around to a few of the schoolchildren. No one recognized her.

We found the main office and asked to speak to the headmaster. "He's out," the secretary told us. "Why do you want to see him?"

"We'd like to speak to him about giving a talk at his school." We were told to wait in the reception area. A few minutes later, the deputy headmaster asked us into his office.

"So how can I help you?" he asked.

"We would like to speak to your students about the Bahá'í Faith," I began. "We are Bahá'ís from America and we try to speak at as many secondary schools as possible here in Botswana."

"I see." He opened a calendar to the second week of October. "How long will you be in Maun?"

Ed shrugged his shoulders and made a wild guess. "A week?"

"Ah, yes then. We would love to have you speak to the students here. What I will do is announce at assembly that visitors from America will be speaking about the Bahá'í Faith after school. Many children do sports then; but some will come, I am certain, to hear what you have to say. On what day shall I make arrangements for you to speak?" We answered that today was just fine, and with a final handshake, we departed.

That afternoon when the schoolchildren saw us waiting at an outdoor lecture area, they approached us half shyly and half curiously, giggling behind small hands. Most of the children were Christians, and spoke English well since they had been taught the language in school when they were very young. They asked questions, referring to quotes from the Bible, especially those dealing with the coming of prophets. One boy, no older than fifteen, was particularly agitated. He was angry that we had the audacity to waltz into town, singing the praises of a man other than Jesus.

"How do we know that this man, Bahá'u'lláh, is not a false prophet warned about in the Bible?" he asked, looking around him for support from his peers. "Jesus said that only through him could the world be saved. He said nothing about this Bahá'u'lláh who you say is the Return." Pounding the Bible which sat on his lap, he exclaimed, "Nothing!"

Though Ed and I had both been involved in the presentation, at this point I stepped back and let him do the difficult task of drawing an understandable parallel between the Biblical references of the return of Jesus and the revelation of Bahá'u'lláh. It didn't go smoothly. Ed's calm demeanor was unruffled as he explained the Bahá'í interpretation of Christ's promise that He would return in a new name, and in the "Glory of the Father," tying it to the English translation of Bahá'u'lláh's name: "the Glory of God." The student rebutted him continually with quotes from the Bible about false prophets. If it had gone on like this – back and forth, back and forth – for only a few minutes I may have been able to control myself. But after twenty minutes I snapped.

"Look," I said. "We're not going to stand here and argue with you so you'll believe what we believe. We've given you the message. Our job is over. We came here to tell you about the Promised One. You've been told. Now it's up to you to take it or leave it. Are there any other questions?" The young boy drew back as if he'd been slapped. At the time, I thought myself quite brave for coming to the rescue of Ed and of my religion, both of which were being ridiculed. It certainly seemed to suppress dissension in the crowd. A few girls raised their hands and quietly asked about the Bahá'í belief in the Trinity and other prophets of God. As Ed answered their questions, I leaned against the chalk board and scanned the crowd for clues as to their reaction to what I'd just said. It wasn't until then that I noticed the change in their faces. When we first entered the room, their faces had been open and welcoming. Now they appeared to be masked with resentment and bitterness. My words had slammed shut a door somewhere, and it hadn't just barred entry from our side; it had barred it from their side as well.

Later that evening, I asked Ed how he felt about the comments I had made. He didn't say anything for a few moments, and I wondered if he'd been questioning the wisdom of my words as much as I had. Teaching the Faith to Christians could sometimes be a daunting task. Though they were anticipating the return of Jesus, after so many generations of waiting, that anticipation had seemed to calcify, leaving one to wonder how best to approach them. There were so many stories demonstrating

Bahá'u'lláh and "Abdu'l-Bahá's methods for teaching the Bahá'í Faith to others, I was often at a loss as to which to apply to what situation. On one hand, we were told to give the message "as a gift to a king," but then we were also admonished not to throw pearls before swine. Instinctively, I knew that each situation called for a different approach, and as I became more engaged in the teaching work, and spiritually developed, the correct remedy would present itself.

When Ed finally did speak, his words surprised me. If he had been disheartened by the way I reacted, he didn't mention it. Instead, he focused on the possible benefits of the experience.

"I was actually happy you said what you did, Kemba. Those kids needed to know that we were more than just two soft-spoken American teenagers. They needed to know that we had backbone. And it was especially important that you were the one who said it."

"Why?"

"Because you're the woman and they probably thought, before then, that you were just my sidekick, or my maid, or something even worse!" Ed was right about that. Several times while in Botswana with my white American or British friends, people had made comments that made their assumptions as to the sexual nature of our relationship quite obvious. They assumed that I was the maid or the girlfriend traveling with my white boss to keep his clothes clean, his belly full, and who knows what else? It was important that these people should see men and women enjoying friendship as equals, where one wasn't subservient to the other, and where sex played no part.

Ed asked the deputy headmaster, when we saw him again after our talk, if he knew of a place we could stay for a few days. We had already spent one night in the only hotel accessible from Maun on foot. We couldn't afford to stay there again. The unexpected cost of plane tickets from South Africa to Namibia a few weeks before had so depleted our savings, we were reducing costs by replacing meals with tinned fruit and greasy chips.

"I'll tell you what," the deputy headmaster said slowly. "I will find the headmaster when he returns from his meeting this afternoon and talk to him. There might be a place where you can stay. Will you meet me here in an hour?"

He returned with the headmaster, who offered us a vacated teacher's house on the edge of the school grounds. We were excited to have been so lucky. He gave us a key, and we moved our bags in that evening.

We finally met Jacqueline at Maun Secondary School (MSS), a few miles outside town. A young girl on the school grounds had recognized Jacqueline's picture when we showed it to her, and ran to get her. Jacqueline walked out a few minutes later.

"*Dumela rra,*" she said, taking Ed's hand. Turning to me, she grasped my hand and said, "*Dumela mma.* How are you?" We spoke briefly about our stay with her brother, and our time with Alan. Then we told her about our appointment to speak at her school later that afternoon, and our delegate election meeting at seven that evening. We didn't see her again until Ed and I stood in front of a group of students at the after-school meeting.

We'd spoken at the religious studies classes earlier that day at MSS, when the students had acted with reverence and respect in the presence of their teachers, hands folded neatly on top of their mahogany tables. But there were no teachers in the room the headmaster allowed us to use for our after-school meeting. The students probed us with one question after another, not waiting until one was answered before they shouted another, mocking the message we'd come to bring. We received questions which displayed a feigned interest in why we had come to Africa in the first place, and suggestions that we go back to America with our "false prophet" and books that were not from the Bible.

Ed was answering the students' shouts and accusations with an even temper and calm words when Jacqueline jumped in. She answered the questions and accusations of her classmates with her head held high, and a clear, steady voice.

Then the language switched from English to Setswana. When a voice laced with sarcasm conspicuous enough even for non-Setswana speakers to hear, shouted something from the audience, Jacqueline would stand up, hands on hips, meeting her classmates' remarks with answers that would draw both laughter and reflection from the crowd. Their shouting gradually subsided until there was only one person speaking: Jacqueline. Alone, she had been able to accomplish what I had seen groups of veteran STAR volunteers fail to do – win the respect and sincere attention of her young audience.

As we left the school grounds Jacqueline accepted, with bowed head and shy smile, our thanks for her assertiveness in the classroom.

"No, really," she insisted, "it was nothing. I get that kind of treatment every time I open my mouth about the Bahá'í Faith."

"What about the Bahá'ís in Maun?" I asked, wondering if she had a supportive community to keep her going. "Have you been meeting with them?"

"Just like you and Ed, I haven't been able to find any of them. And I really have searched. But what I do have is enough to keep me going: a prayer book and a copy of *The Light of Bahá'u'lláh*. Do not worry about me, friends! I have what I need."

It was dark when we finished cleaning the house for the delegate election meeting that was to begin at seven. The house we had borrowed was small, so there wasn't much to do besides sweep the concrete floor free of bugs and sand, and arrange and re-arrange the three chairs. Ed left a little before seven to wait by the school gates for the Bahá'ís. He returned a little past eight, smiling despite his tiredness. Following close behind were two men. They were tall and lean, their clothes in tatters. I offered them seats and introduced myself.

Holding my hand to my chest I bowed slightly as I had seen other Batswana do.

"Eh?"

"They only speak Setswana," Jacqueline said. Then she introduced us, in Setswana, to the two men. They sat stiffly in the chairs, as if they weren't used to the cushions.

We only had a few Bahá'í books left after presenting so many to school libraries. We gave the men some of our remaining ones. While they looked through the books, I opened my copy of *Bahá'í Readings* to that day's date, 13 October, and found this passage:

How great, how very great is the Cause! How very fierce the onslaught of all the peoples and kindreds of the earth. Ere long shall the clamour of the multitude throughout Africa, throughout America, the cry of the European and of the Turk, the groaning of India and China, be heard from far and near. One and all, they shall arise with all their power to resist His Cause. Then shall the knights of the Lord, assisted by His Grace from on high, strengthened by faith, aided by the power of understanding, and reinforced by the legions of the Covenant, arise and make manifest the truth of the verse: "Behold the confusion that hath befallen the tribes of the defeated!"

'Abdu'l-Bahá

That evening, 'Abdu'l-Bahá's words touched me in a way they never had before. They perfectly matched what we had encountered all week from schoolchildren: an onslaught of resistance. His words also reflected how we had tried to arise and share a spiritual truth, despite their attempts to pull us down.

As I sat in that tiny room in Maun, listening to Jacqueline and Ed explain the relevance of *The Light of Bahá'u'lláh*, copies of which they'd given the two men, I felt a happiness overcome me from deep within. I was certain that we were truly teaching Bahá'u'lláh's Cause. I had never before felt so happy and complete.

It was at times like these that I most strongly felt the conviction in my decision to become a Bahá'í. That decision had been slow in coming. It hadn't mattered that I was raised in a Bahá'í family; every individual is encouraged to independently investigate the truth for themselves. For those raised in Bahá'í families, this investigation usually precedes the age of maturity, fifteen, the earliest age an official declaration of one's religious preference can be made. For some, this is a smooth transition; the parents are delighted, friends approve, life continues unabated. But then there are cases like mine.

On my fifteenth birthday, while my parents and brother tiptoed around the house hoping – praying! – for a miracle, I made an announcement. Not only was I not going to be a Bahá'í, I wasn't going to belong to any of the other religions I'd looked into, either. Just as I'd once wanted nothing to do with Africa, I now wanted nothing to do with religion. I rather liked the sound of "agnostic".

You see, no one had ever told me that I could be a Bahá'í without imitating the way my parents were Bahá'ís. I didn't realize that for every individual there's a unique way of being a Bahá'í. What I did know was that I didn't want to be public figures like my parents, always giving lectures on this or that topic, always *en route* to this place or that. I was, by nature, a quite and contemplative person, and I wanted to be a Bahá'í quietly.

What I'm describing in a few lines took years to register, and is part of the reason why discovering my role became so important to me in Southern Africa. Luckily, I wasn't left alone at fifteen to begin this process. The sunlit living room with the rubber tree in the corner was put to good use again, this time to convince me of another truth. And, just as before, Dad sat me down for what was going to be his last attempt. He was getting too old for this, and believe it or not, "agnostic" sounded a whole lot better than "heart attack at forty-eight". But it wasn't just the story of "raising the stones" that did it; it was his rendition of the future concerning me and my baby brother. And if our sibling relationship had been any different, even this last attempt would have failed, but our relationship was special; I had taught Ali how to read before kindergarten, how to make board games out of cardboard scraps and magic markers, and how to cheat at washing the dishes by hiding dirty pots in the oven. I was his mentor! So when Dad sat me down in that living room and told me that if I didn't grab on to Bahá'u'lláh's revelation He would "raise the stones" to do His work on this earth – meaning in the case of the Thomas family, that He would raise up my baby brother to surpass me – the fear of God took hold.

Now, I'm not saying that the fear of Ali being spiritually raised above me was the best (or worse) reason for finally deciding to become a Bahá'í, nor am I saying that this fear alone is what did it. Rather, it was the last straw that broke the camel's back. It caused me to open my eyes, and take a deeper look at this religion and to see what had been there all along, just waiting to be discovered.

The men had many questions to ask about the Bahá'í Faith. During the course of the evening, we learned more and more about our visitors. They had walked fourteen kilometers from their village to meet us, and had brought with them the delegate election forms filled out by all the Bahá'ís of their village:a neatly folded pile that they took from deep within their pockets and placed on the coffee table. Only one of the two men was a registered Bahá'í. The tall man placed his hand on his friend's shoulder, and turned to speak again to Jacqueline.

"The other man walked fourteen kilometers just to hear the word of God," Jacqueline translated for us. I looked up at the small man thumbing through his copy of *The Light of Bahá'u'lláh*. He held it in his hands as if it were a fragile flower that he feared would be crushed.

It was getting late and the two men had a long journey ahead of them, so they left after a short while. Ed was going to walk Jacqueline back to MSS, but before they could leave the school grounds, one of Jacqueline's teachers stopped on his way home from a party and offered her a lift. She climbed into the car with a smile and a wave and disappeared into the darkness.

Next morning, we left for Nata.

A woman from the bar where we were dropped off, on the edge of the village, recognized Gakeatsalwa Gasane's name and immediately took us to her. Gasane was our contact in Nata. She'd been told weeks before of our visit. The woman from the bar took us down a path with rondavaals comfortably spaced on either side. As children saw Ed and me, and the large backpacks we carried, they jumped up and down shouting, "Good morning, teacher!"

Gasane stood in her yard as we approached, wiping her hands on a rag. She motioned for us to sit on wooden stumps while she cleaned out a rondavaal for us to sleep in. Lifting both our heavy backpacks at once, and laughing as their weight pulled her down, she placed them in the newly cleaned room.

The moment I set eyes on Gasane, there was something very special about her that made me feel sad; sad because I knew that in a few days I'd have to leave her. I recognized in Gasane a spark of my own mother's spirit, just as I had recognized the same in Mrs Semela, and in many other people I'd come across during my journey through Africa. I never felt very far from my parents, because I could see them in so many of the faces around me. Mrs Semela was the first to make me realize the existence of a kind of universal parenthood.

Often, when writing home, I tried to explain this idea to my parents. It must have seemed odd to them to read my letters, stating that even though we were separated by the Atlantic Ocean, I could still find traces of them everywhere: a school principal in South Africa, a village woman in Nata, a pioneer family in Gaborone, an old woman in Mozambique. I was never without parents to help guide me through my physical and spiritual journeys.

Later that same day we met Tot. He was a small, stout youth whose eyes stayed fixed on the ground when he spoke. Ed had asked him where the Bahá'ís were, and Tot had pointed to three far-off places in turn. At our request, he agreed to take us to see the closest ones. There were five, all women, very excited to see their names in print on our list. One Bahá'í, with a bright turquoise and brown cloth wrapped around her head, greeted us with a warm smile as we walked into her yard. Then Tot told her that we were Bahá'ís from America.

"I am no longer Bahá'í," she said when she spoke again. Her voice trembled with anger. "You people took too long to come and see me again, and I changed churches."

"I apologize mma, for the Bahá'ís failing to come and see you more often," Ed said, bowing humbly.

"There are so few of us that can travel like we do," I added pointing to Ed and myself, "and there are so many Bahá'ís to visit in so many different villages."

"Well, as I said, I have changed churches." Turning around, she walked away and left us standing in her yard. On our way to see the next Bahá'í, we discussed where this view of the Bahá'í Faith having "missionaries" who visit the people to reinforce their faith came from. Though the Bahá'í community strives to be supporting, loving and enriching, one's faith in God shouldn't depend on the behavior of other members of the community. Only the Faith itself is perfect, the Bahá'í community is not.

The last woman we found was lying beneath a pile of blankets in front of her rondavaal, her voice no more than a whisper. Tot, listening closely to what she said, told us that she was very ill. But still she found the energy to get up and bring us chairs to sit on.

She wasn't sure if she'd be well enough to make it to our election meeting the next evening, she said, but she could vote right now. We said a healing prayer for her, and left her beneath her blankets.

On the way back to Gasane's home, I looked at the list of Bahá'ís and noticed that there were a few people we hadn't seen yet. I asked Tot about them. A few had moved away, some were at their lands. Another was Tot's father, whom he told us we wouldn't be able to see because he was "late". "He's late?" I repeated. "Well, we can wait to see him, can't we? How late will he be?" Tot looked embarrassed.

"It is impossible for you to see him, because he is late," he said again slowly, pronouncing each word carefully.

"Let me tell you something, Tot," I said, winking at Ed. "Bahá'ís are always late. If a meeting is supposed to start at eight, you can show up at eight-thirty without having missed a thing. We call it 'Bahá'í time' back home." Tot took in a deep breath and prepared to speak again.

Ed caught on to what Tot meant before I did. Grabbing my arm he whispered, "No, Kemba. Tot means his father has passed away. Dead. That's what he meant by 'late'."

"Oh goodness," I tried to hide my embarrassment behind an upraised hand. "Sorry Tot," I whispered, but Tot wasn't there to hear me. He was already walking down the path that lead to Gasane's.

The next morning, I awoke to the sound of Gasane's voice, which had eased its way into my sleep. When I went outside, she gave a loud *"Dumela mma!"* and spoke quickly in Setswana. The only other word I recognized was *"ta ta"* which meant "a lot." Gasane leaned her head on her hands, mimicking sleep. I smiled and looked at my watch. It was only eight o'clock and she was telling me that I slept a lot! I shook my head and sighed as she gave me practice in Setswana by asking how I was doing, then having me repeat after her.

Gasane didn't speak any English except for a few words such as "dirty", "toilet", and "sit down", and my Setswana wasn't much better. At first I was frustrated because I couldn't understand what she was trying to say, and she couldn't understand me either. Then, at the height of my frustration, when I thought I could take no more, I just let it go like seeds to the wind. I had to let go of my hold on the necessity of words, and with this letting go came peace of mind and a realization that time didn't have to be filled up with words. There were other ways to communicate, other ways to understand. Slowly, I began to open up to what was going on around me by using my other senses. Between Gasane and me there were very few words, but we still grew to understand and love one another.

I spent that day following Gasane around like a lost child. Together we went to the well, where we pumped water into buckets, then carried them home on our heads. Gasane hooted in laughter as my bucket tipped and spilled water down my back, staining the dry earth bright red. Later on that day, moving to a beat in her head, she rhythmically pounded sorghum in a hollow log to a fine consistency. When mixed with water, the ground sorghum would make a thick porridge.

Bahá'ís arrived for the meeting hours before it was to begin. So much for my American idea about "Bahá'í time"! A goat skin was laid out in the shade from the cooking hut where the sorghum was boiling to thickness in a black cauldron. First to arrive was a slim old lady dressed in fancy hat and shoes. She sat beside Gasane as she tended to the cooking. "*Dumela mma*," she said when she caught sight of me sitting on the goat skin and writing in my journal.

"*Dumela mma*," I replied, and then added, "*Ots wo heely?*" like Gasane had taught me. The woman in the fancy hat chuckled to herself and looked up at Gasane, who stood there looking proud.

Next came Tot, who immediately got into a conversation with Ed about Shoghi Effendi. He wanted to know everything there was to know about the Guardian. Tot's questions lasted longer than Ed's answers. When I looked at him closely, I realized that Tot was drunk.

"I know . . . I know that you are disappointed in me," he began, his head rolling back and forth on his thick neck. "I know you are disappointed in me because I am drunk. And I know that you know I am drunk," he said with a wry smile. "But life is such that I had no choice."

"What do you mean?" I asked.

"You see that lady sitting there?" He pointed toward an old lady who smiled flirtatiously back at Tot. "Because my brother died – who was her husband – I now have to marry her." Then he whispered in a thick and heavy voice, "It is the custom."

"But Tot, she is old enough to be your mother!" I exclaimed.

"I know," Tot said, his eyes drifting toward the heavens. "Why do you think I am drunk?"

The meeting began. We sang songs and read prayers, stopping only to eat, and, later, to cast votes. Tot was in no condition to translate, so Ed and I stepped back and watched the meeting take its own shape. Bahá'ís had come from all around. Some came from their lands, where they farmed in large fields miles outside the village, and there were a few Bahá'ís that we had seen earlier in the week. I was surprised to see the lady who had announced to us that she was no longer a Bahá'í. At first she sat at the edge of the group, as if unsure whether to join us. As the evening passed into night and the singing grew more lively, she inched closer and closer. When she finally sat among us, the plate of biscuits was passed to her and Gasane gave her a welcoming smile. It felt good to be in a Bahá'í community again, and to recognize similar patterns and characters to those in my Bahá'í community back home. Here, in the middle of Botswana, there were some who served as pillars of their community, and others who were lukewarm, with one foot in the Faith, the other somewhere else.

It was comforting for me to see these familiar patterns, because it made me realize that though there may be large cultural differences between one Bahá'í community and another, they also have their obvious similarities. Whether a Bahá'í community is based in a village or a city, it is still a group of individuals struggling to follow Bahá'u'lláh's teachings, and trying to build a community based on Bahá'í ideals.

*

It was an afternoon when nothing much was going on. Ed and Tot had gone to the store to buy crisps, and I was stretched out on a goatskin watching some neighbors dig a hole in the ground. They were building a well, I'd been told.

"Kemba!" Gasane taped me on the shoulder, "Come," she pointed to the rondavaal where all her belongings lay tucked away in cupboards and boxes. "Come." I followed her into the room, sitting down beside her on a small couch. She removed a box from a corner and withdrew a small collection of letters. Carefully, she unwrapped the string tied around it. She placed two cards on my lap. They were sympathy cards with pictures of angels and clouds. Inside were short messages, written in English:

Gasane, we are very sorry to have heard the news that your husband has so suddenly passed away. Our prayers are with you always.

Gasane, we were so saddened by the news. Please accept our sincerest condolences. Your husband was a wonderful friend to us all. Now he is resting peacefully.

She put more cards and letters on my lap. They were from Bahá'ís all over Botswana, offering their sympathies at the passing of her husband. After they had all been read, she gently gathered them together, tucked them back inside their envelopes, and retied the string.

The morning we left Nata for Kasane, the last village where we were to help with the delegate elections, Tot sat with us at the side of the road as we waited for a lift. He was quieter than the previous day, when alcohol had loosened his tongue. He was worried about being the only Bahá'í (apart from Gasane), in Nata. We asked him about the other Bahá'ís who attended the meeting. "They are only Bahá'ís when other Bahá'ís come to town," he said. He told us that his father had always wanted him to be a good Bahá'í, and to study the writings of Shoghi Effendi, but he hadn't listened. And now his father was gone. Ed and I looked at each other, and then at Tot sitting with his head bowed nearly in his lap.

"You have to be strong, Tot. Bahá'u'lláh never said it would be easy. It's not supposed to be easy," I said. Tot let out a little sigh. A large white and yellow Mack truck stopped at the petrol station across the street, and Ed ran over to see if we could get a lift to Kasane. I looked at Tot sitting there, just a few years older than I, and was reminded of Jacqueline, another youth who had to struggle to keep the flame lit within her own heart.

"Put your trust in Bahá'u'lláh," I said, "not in the Bahá'ís around you. Bahá'u'lláh is the only one who belongs in your heart."

We went in the Mack truck, leaving Tot sitting by the side of the road, mustering a smile he only let show on special occasions. When I asked about the brown mounds lying on the road that was paved and smooth, our driver explained to us the art of driving in a land full of elephants.

"It's hard to see them," he said while scanning the forest to either side of him, "because they're gray like the trees." The trees, bearing very few leaves, were really more of a brownish colour. But at the speed we were going, they did seem to blur into a grayish tone. Then the truck driver quickly tapped my leg and drew my attention to something on our left. It was so well hidden, that at first all I saw was a tree. Then I saw the elephant, its trunk and front leg raised high in the air, its skin a gentle gray. Though it must have only been seconds, it seemed to stand still for eternity. I took in every wrinkle of its skin, every fold, every surrounding branch, as slowly and clearly as a photograph. When my attention returned to the conversation inside the truck, I heard the driver tell Ed that what we saw was only a small elephant. Yet it had been larger than anything I had ever seen in a zoo.

He told us how local police officers had decided to disable the horns in tourists' cars. Previously, if tourists forgot the police's warnings not to honk their horns, or did so by accident . . . the noise could be heard for a mile's radius. To elephant mothers, a honking horn sounds like the cry of a baby elephant in distress. So the mother comes running toward the sound, and sees the car innocently driving down the road. When elephant mothers think their babies are in danger, they see everything as a threat, and that's where the tourist's ride can come to an abrupt end. Sometimes the cars, flattened like coins, aren't found for days.

"That's why I don't drive these roads at night," he said. We moved on to other topics of conversation, but my mind stayed on elephants for some time and I kept searching for the sight of another one until the driver dropped us off in Kasane.

There was a large sign on the outskirts of Kasane indicating that Victoria Falls was ninety-three kilometers to the east, and Kasane three kilometers straight ahead. Ed and I stood studying the sign, wondering which way to go. To the people of Southern Africa, Victoria Falls was known as *Mosi oa Tunya*, "The Smoke that Thunders." Though I'd never heard of it back in the States, the Youth Service Corps volunteers in Botswana talked about it all the time. I had seen pictures of the waterfall, but I'd been told that the pictures didn't do justice to it. To truly experience Victoria Falls, you had to feel the spray from the abyss like rain, even on the hottest days, and hear the rumbling like a volcano vibrate the very earth.

We'd lived like nomads for four weeks, covering more than five thousand kilometers over three countries. Traveling around Southern Africa, our only belongings strapped to our backs, with whole countries ours to explore, gave us a sense of freedom and detachment. Yet, Ed and I still longed for a break from the uncertainties and fatigue of travel. This is why the 93 kilometers to Victoria Falls, a tourist town with hotels and restaurants, looked tempting, although our last village for delegate elections was only a few miles away.

"Well, what should we do?" I asked Ed. "I need a vacation, a meal, and a shower."

"I definitely agree. You do need a shower."

"Cut it out, Ed. I'm serious."

Ed squinted his eyes in thought for a moment. "Here's a plan," he said, tentatively. "We could either spend a full week in Kasane and forget about seeing the seventh wonder of the world, which we're so close to now, or we could spend a few days doing both."

We pondered our options for a few minutes. I felt a little

selfish having said that I needed a rest from travel-teaching and visiting Bahá'ís. Wasn't I here to serve the needs of the Bahá'í community? But I couldn't serve to my full potential if I was so mentally and physically exhausted, could I? I thought back with a laugh to the last time I'd tried to get to the Falls. It had been two-and-a-half months before, when I left for Victoria Falls with Corey and Briar. The whole day had been one great race against the clock. We had raced to get to the hitch-hiking post on the outskirts of Gaborone in the morning, raced to make the Botswana/Zimbabwe border by mid-afternoon, so that we could then make the seven o'clock train to Victoria Falls. It was 5.30 when we got to the border north of Francistown. We had ninety minutes to pass the border and find a ride to Bulawayo, where we were to catch the train. I was so frantic while filling out my exit forms, I kept fumbling with my pen, making indecipherable scribbles. I was nervous as I approached the man who was asking questions and stamping passports and travel papers. It was my first time out of Botswana alone without Uncle Louie or any other adult to sweet talk the officials through any problems.

After I showed him my passport, the border official wanted to see my temporary residence permit. The slip of paper I fished out of my hip pouch didn't satisfy him. It was only a receipt proving that I had applied for stay inside Botswana three times. Where was the actual paper permitting my stay? Then I realized the importance of being taken to the immigration office time and time again to get my permit. I wasn't legal without it, nor did I have the right to leave Botswana. Briar and Corey were already through the line. They stood halfway out the door looking back at me, wondering what the problem was.

The immigration officer asked to see my plane ticket back to the States to prove that I had a way out of Botswana. I had taken it out of my pouch and locked it in my suitcase just that morning: my suitcase back in Gaborone.

"So what do you want me to do?" I said, fighting back my anger. "We've got to make our seven o'clock train. I don't carry my plane tickets around with me. Its too risky!" Especially on vacation – who would?

"I don't care about you making your train," he answered. "I can't let you through until you can prove that you can get back into Botswana." I looked up at him in shock, summoning up my courage to do some negotiating. But before I could utter another word, he slid my passport to my side of the counter and asked for the next person in line. Two hours later, Briar, Corey and I were camping out in a wide field beneath the stars in no man's land, between the borders of Botswana and Zimbabwe. The borders had closed before we could solve the problem, so we had to stay here until they re-opened. Luckily, we were prepared. We had sleeping bags, candles, fresh rolls, hard salami, pocket knives, handy wipes, a cassette player and plenty of tapes. I made plates out of paper from my journal, and we ate sandwiches by candle-light.

The following morning we parted: Briar and Corey went north-east to catch the train from Bulawayo, and I headed back to Gaborone. Briar didn't want me to go back on my own. Neither of us had ever traveled alone before, especially a distance such as the 465 kilometers back to Gaborone, but she was returning to the States in a month. Seeing Victoria Falls was her African dream. I couldn't deprive her of that. I started trembling even before a friendly taxi driver stuffed me into his already stuffed cab. He carried on about the injustice of the immigration officers while driving me back to the Botswana side of the border. Although I laughed and joked with him, retelling my story to the captive audience in the cab, I was truly frightened. I had to travel across Botswana for the first time alone.

The only real hassle I had was from the guards at the Botswana border post. They stopped me at the blue and white-striped pole which marked the border line, and searched me. While they went though my backpack, reading letters friends back home had sent (and laughing), I stared stony-eyed at the jagged hills of Zimbabwe I was leaving behind. It was early morning and the clouds were splashed orange and pink. I remember wondering if I'd ever make it back to this beautiful land, so different from the desert to which I was returning.

Ed and I decided to stay in Kasane for two days and then go to

Victoria Falls. On our list of the Bahá'ís of Kasane, there was a man named Martin, a nurse, so we went straight to the local hospital to find him. We must have looked tired. As soon as Martin saw us he wanted to take us to his home to rest. He led us out to the parking lot and stopped, with his hands in the air.

"Well, where is it?" he asked, looking back and forth at Ed and me.

"Where is what?" I asked.

"Where is your vehicle? Don't you guys have a vehicle?" Martin looked shocked as we shook our heads. "You've come all this way on foot?" His look changed to disbelief as we nodded our heads. "My God!" he said slowly, kicking the ground. "Then it will be a long walk to my place."

In previous years, the STAR project had "youth-mobiles": vehicles donated to the volunteers to use for delegate elections, teaching trips, and other services to the Cause. This was the first year with no youth-mobiles. Too many had been crashed, we were told. People were amazed to see Bahá'í youth from Europe and America traveling to their villages without a vehicle. We were on foot, like most of the African people, instead of behaving like stereotypical rich Westerners.

Martin led us through a section of the village with homes of stacked metal and cardboard. Women chattered while washing clothes in large plastic buckets. Men and small children on bicycles wound between rocks and beer cans, pounded into the earth. We stopped in front of Martin's home, and he asked us to wait a moment while he straightened up inside. I sat in a chair beneath some shade, watching life buzz around us. In a clearing a few yards away, boys in striped black and white shirts played soccer. They were still playing when, later on, three Bahá'ís from Kasane, Ed and I sat in a circle outside Martin's house. The sun had gone down and a single candle flickered in one young Bahá'í's hand as he said a prayer. After prayers, we sang – quietly at first, our voices blending in with the passing breeze. Then as darkness came, our voices grew louder and louder.

Martin shook our hands the next day as we left for Zimbabwe. "I am still sad to see you go," he said, "but I know what it is like when a person needs a few days vacation time.

Please come back if you can." We promised we'd try. He found us a lift to the border. The man who drove us was in the middle of making a delivery. The back of his truck was filled with cans of paint, a ladder, tools, and a large wooden book shelf. Everything slid to one side as we rounded corners, and I looked behind me nervously, as Ed and Martin held on for dear life.

There were two hitch-hikers' backpacks sitting outside the border office: one bright turquoise, the other bright orange. "Looks like we have some competition," I said as we unstrapped our packs and laid them beside the others. I saw the hitch-hikers through an open door of the office while filling out my entry forms. They stood near a fence on the other side of the border, looking down the road toward Zimbabwe. A few minutes later they approached us with a tempting proposition.

"We've just called a cab to take us to Vic Falls," the first one said.

"We've been waiting here since the border opened at seven, and no one has come through," the other one sighed. He scratched his brow and shook his hair out of his face. It was a white blond, like his friend's. I looked at my watch. It was around ten o'clock. "Why don't you join us and we'll split the cost four ways. It's 78 'zim-dollars' total."

"Sounds good to me, when is it coming?" Ed asked. Just then a cab with "Victoria Falls" hand-painted on the side pulled up and honked. I quickly explained our "zim-dollar" currency predicament: we didn't have any. They agreed to take Pula, Botswana's currency, and we hopped into the cab.

The hitch-hikers were Swedish medical students, spending their college vacation touring Southern Africa. They had only good things to say about Zimbabwe, insisting that it was the cheapest, friendliest, and most beautiful country in Southern Africa. They told us that they'd driven through Wanki Game Park seeing all kinds of game, and had rented a small cottage for only ten Zimbabwean dollars. Their eyes lit up as each one tried to finish telling the story. Laughing at their own eagerness, the man in the front sat back and let his friend speak. They had rented a small 4x4, but they didn't really need it in Zimbabwe.

"The roads aren't like those in Botswana!" he said. Even the cab driver laughed at that revelation. "Plus, everything is so much cheaper than Botswana."

"We went to the Okavango Delta in Botswana, and could only afford to stay for one day! But here in Zimbabwe, we can stay for practically nothing."

I looked at Ed and smiled. "Well then, I guess we've come to the right place."

The town of Victoria Falls was just as I'd expected: small, and just walking distance from the Falls itself. Tourists, in shorts and sunglasses, walked hand-in-hand or rode past on rented bicycles.

We spent no more than an hour at the edge of the Falls. The paths leading to the Falls were filled with vines and trees, their leaves blocking the light of the sun, and tinting the air around us green. Every few yards, the path would dip along the edge of the cliff and the Falls sounded like thunder; a fine mist, thick as smoke, filled the air. Smoke that thundered. The size of the Falls was amazing: a gigantic crack in the earth stretching far on either side. In the right light, you could see rainbows.

An hour or so later, the initial excitement having worn off, we were left wandering around the small town wondering what else it had to offer two financially embarrassed people such as ourselves. The medical students had told us about the Victoria Falls hotel. It was a "must see". When we got there, I understood why. The hotel had polished floors, spiral stairways, and courtyards with fountains and flowers. In the lobby were malachite carvings of abstract figurines, amongst which men in white and black uniforms served lunch. Behind the hotel, a path led to the Falls, and to a playground occupied by baby monkeys eating fruit which had fallen from the trees. A man in his mid-50s stood with us as we watched the monkeys play and squabble like little children.

"Beautiful, isn't it?" he said softly after we'd been watching them for some time. "I've watched them come out here every morning and early evening since I've been here. There's not much else to do after you've seen the falls a few hundred times."

"Tell me about it," I said. "This is our first day, and we've already run out of cheap things to do." The chalet which we'd rented for twenty-seven Zimbabwean dollars a day had a bulletin board advertising horseback tours around the Falls, champagne breakfasts, and white water rafting. But none of these activities were as cheap as the entrance fee to the Falls.

That evening we had our first proper meal in days. We both put on the best clothes we had, and walked back to the Victoria Falls Hotel. We weren't admitted into the hotel restaurant. Our clothes were wrinkled and stained from travel, and the stiff-necked *maitre d'* told us that the dress code of the restaurant was just short of black tie. Then where could we go to get a decent meal, we asked. The barbecue out back, he suggested. He showed us the way. This was something far removed from the family barbecues I had experienced back home. Chefs in tall, skinny, white hats cooked and served ribs, roast beef, potatoes, ham and steaks, over long narrow grills. Round tables with lighted candles were dotted around the courtyard, and soft music played.

The next day, we left Victoria Falls. We'd had enough relaxation and pampering to keep us going for a few more weeks in the teaching field. I had hopes of coming back to Victoria Falls – with money – so I could do all the things I couldn't do the first time. But as fate would have it, I never did return.

*

16 October

Kemba,

I can't believe it has taken me this long to get this letter off! As usual, I'm feeling swamped, saying prayers everyday for radiance and servitude. But otherwise, everything is going well. We had a wonderful two or three month session on the Kitáb-i-Íqán that all the Bahá'í club folk came to. At the end two non-Bahá'ís who had been coming declared, plus the Bahá'ís who came have a new

65

appreciation of that book; I'm sure I do! It was heartwarming to see that it could help two people find their way into the Faith.

Anyway, I wanted to remind you, while you are there, to really use this opportunity to help you chart out your career choices. Certainly, you want to have some major in mind when you start university.

It is a wonderful step forward that you have chosen literature as your first love. I've always loved literature too, and although I know we tend to think of your dad as the writer of the family, the truth is that I would really rather do nothing more than write, and that is the part of my job that I like the most.

The most important thing about your career area is that it must be something that you like to do, or rather that you love to do. Then you will be willing to put the time into it that would be necessary to really master the craft of writing, not just the mechanics of grammar, but the craft of writing in which you are showing such promise.

However, I hope that you are taking the opportunity to critically think about how you can mesh a life's work that you really enjoy with service to mankind. You know that Bahá'u'lláh has said many things about this. For example, in His Tablet of Glad-Tidings, Bishárát, He says:

> "It is enjoined upon every one of you to engage in some form of occupation, such as crafts, trades and the like. We have graciously exalted your engagement in such work to the rank of worship unto God, the True One. . . . Waste not your time in idleness and sloth. Occupy yourselves with that which profiteth yourselves and others. . . ."

You have read enough novels to know that while some of the writing meets these standards, some does not. We really need writers that can give us hope, vision and transcend minute characterizations of negative things! Here is where you could really make a contribution.

66

Take extra special care of yourself. I miss you so badly it hurts. I hope that you are having a tremendously positive experience, and keeping your health up. We are going through some rough times trying to figure out expenses; can we expect to see you home before your brother's birthday in February?

Mom

The skeleton of a great warrior

When I phoned my parents to ask them if I could go to Mozambique for a month, the request was slipped in with a myriad other accounts of my adventures, so they hardly knew what hit them. "Can you go to Mozambique? Oh sure honey! Now let's get back to that thrilling story about when you were caught between the borders of Botswana and Zimbabwe for the night!" They didn't find out what Mozambique was really all about, in terms of the war that had been raging there for many years, until I was relatively safe and back in the States. My mother had watched a television special on PBS about the homeless children of war in Mozambique. A few hours later, her face was still ashen. She asked me to tell her what I saw and felt and experienced there, and over the course of the next few days, I did. But first, each story had to be sifted through my consciousness, before it could be properly told and shared. Whenever I felt a story budding within me, which was usually on the long car drives I took with my mother across country, when hours slipped by uncounted, then a story would become ready to be told.

The whole trip was Motshedi's idea. She approached me in mid-August when all the youth volunteers were planning teaching trips in Namibia, South Africa and the villages of Botswana, that she couldn't join because of her studies.

"KT," she said one morning as we sat around the Kays' oak table in Gaborone, listening to Uncle Louie's old Roberta Flack tapes, "I want to go on a teaching trip. We should go on one together, just the two of us."

"Sure," I answered somewhat hesitantly. My next few

months were already filled with teaching trips and delegate elections. "When were you thinking about going?" She had holidays in January and the first half of February. I was planning to go back to the States around that time, so if this did work out, it would be my last teaching trip in Africa. When I asked her where she wanted to go, I was hoping she'd suggest somewhere nice like Swaziland or Zimbabwe.

"Mmm . . . I want to go to a place where I don't know the language . . ." she said dreamily. Motshedi was born and raised in Botswana and could speak both English and Setswana fluently. ". . . I want to go to Mozambique!" My antennae went up. Mozambique's civil war was still all over the newspapers and magazines, despite the fact that it was twenty years old.

"Correct me if I'm wrong," I said slowly, "but isn't there a war or something going on on that side?" She answered that yes, indeed there was a war going on, on that side. Then she began to clean her nails as if the fact of a simple little war didn't bother her in the least.

"Why on earth would you want to go there?"

"Who else needs to hear the message of peace more than they do?" she answered softly.

"Well, can't we just send them a few copies of The Promise of World Peace or something, and add a few more years to our lives?" I was grasping at straws, but I did have a point. Mozambique could be more than just dangerous for our health.

"The Universal House of Justice has requested that travel teachers go to Mozambique," she insisted. I knew she was going to throw a fact like that at me. "Don't worry KT!" she said happily now because she knew she had won, "I'll take care of everything. Money, tickets, visas – everything."

Even then I hadn't quite believed it possible, thinking to myself that this was simply an I'm-going-to-organize-a-teaching-trip-to-war-stricken-Mozambique fad that would eventually fade. But when Motshedi and her father dropped me off at the airport a few months later, I knew for sure that this was no dream. Motshedi's visa hadn't come through yet, and I'd have to fly into Mozambique alone.

I changed flights first at Jan Smuts International airport in

Johannesburg. When I approached the South African Airways desk, I looked properly bewildered at the employee who refused to let me on the plane. I didn't have my visa. Even though it had "come through" it was still in Mozambique, where I was to pick it up at the airport.

"We can't let you onto the plane without your Mozambique visa," he said again.

"Okay." I shrugged my shoulders and tried to look disappointed. I'd just have to tell Motshedi that I tried. Secretly, I was relieved. Even though Motshedi was going to meet me with her visa in Mozambique in what she estimated would take a week, I was still quite uncertain about risking my life. The young SAA employee disappeared into an office behind his desk. When he returned, he told me I'd be allowed on the plane, since I insisted that my visa was waiting for me in Mozambique. But if they found that I had no visa there, I'd be sent back on the next flight.

". . . and they won't be too happy with you," I heard him say as I left for the boarding gate. I hoped that my visa was there, and I worried about this for the whole trip from Johannesburg to Maputo, capital city of Mozambique. The phone lines weren't working from Mozambique to the outside world because of the war. That my visa had come through was only hearsay.

The section of the Maputo airport with customs and passport control was separated from the waiting room by a large glass wall and checkout gates. I watched as the other passengers filled out their pink forms and went to one of several lines. One line was for foreigners and citizens with Mozambique passports, and the other line was for foreigners without Mozambique passports. The last line was moving quickly. That was my line. I stood around for a while waiting for something to happen – a courier paging me with a cardboard sign tied around his neck and my visa in his back pocket, my name sounding over the intercom – anything! Who was supposed to give me my visa, and where were they? I sat down on a leather bench in a corner. To either side of the passport control gates were armed guards, watching everyone's moves. They stood like statues, long rifles hanging down from thin waists.

I looked out beyond the glass wall. A dozen or so people were waiting for friends or relatives on the flight. One by one, I caught the eye of these waiting people, in the hope that one of them would be waiting for someone of my description. But no one was. Their eyes swept pass mine, without a flicker of recognition. I was afraid to go to the passport and customs officer without my visa. As soon as I was discovered to be without it, the best thing I could hope for was to be sent back unharmed. It didn't occur to me until an hour later that my visa might have been waiting with the officer at the gate under my name. It was, in an alphabetized box with dozens of others.

When I looked up from filling out my last form, I saw a middle-aged Indian man searching the crowd from behind a closed gate. I took out the piece of paper where Motshedi had written my contact's name, and mouthed "Rana" at the same time he mouthed my name. An hour later, I was safe inside his gray concrete apartment complex with his wife Veena and their children, answering questions about my travels thus far and laughing to myself at the fear I'd felt just an hour before, its bitter taste still in my mouth.

We'd just finished an Indian meal, with ripe mangoes from the market for dessert, when Mrs Veena Rana told me of the intensity of the problem in Mozambique.

"They are bandits," she began slowly, when I asked about the war. Its effects had caused dark bags like shadows under her eyes, making her look older than her twenty-six years. "Bandits of the other party, not the ruling party, who . . . who harass and even kill people." Then Veena closed her eyes tight, as if in pain. In the distance a steady howling rose in a hellish crescendo. Her baby son found another reason to be annoyed as he played in the guest room with his sister. The guest room was where I was staying during my time with the Ranas. The children found my "American toys" interesting, and often went through my small sewing kit, taking apart the scissors, and playing with the miniature spools of thread so that the room was draped in cobwebs of color. I hoped that the kit wasn't keeping them entertained this time. I had hidden it deep in my bag. Before I could get up to check, Veena spoke again.

71

"They've ambushed nearly all the major roads from city to city or village to village, so it's impossible to get anywhere unless you fly. In the north, it's very dangerous . . ." Then she looked out the window, where a few blocks away lay the sea. I sensed the sea's closeness – the air felt heavy with it. "They raid sometimes whole villages, killing people, maiming people . . ." Mrs Rana continued to speak about Maputo's problems, as the largest city in Mozambique, and its capital. Both these factors also made it the safest. But the war found its own way of slipping through the cracks of Maputo's concrete fortress. The electricity and water lines were often cut from outside the city. Sometimes it took government soldiers weeks to locate the lines that had been tampered with. Then they had to be repaired. Each passing day without water, influenza swept through the city like a bush fire. The government eventually learned to adjust to these problems. When the lines were cut, the remaining water in the lines, and the reserve supply, were rationed out to different parts of the city, one sector at a time. The electric power was switched over to the local power plant, and electricity was also rationed throughout the city. Because the Ranas lived in the diplomatic section of town, we usually had water for a few hours each morning while we waited for the lines to be fixed. The rest of the city wasn't so lucky.

Mozambique was, in a sense, the summation of my journey to Africa. It was my last teaching trip, my last adventure, my last taste of a new country before returning to my own. Africa taught me to think of time, not as an empty space that had to be filled up, or as a gift that had to be opened and seized. It could be gently unwrapped and lingered over. Hours could be spent admiring the sky, or the landscape, or the shape of a rooster atop a fence. And these hours could be spent without guilt that they were being wasted. How can rushing about until we forget to see the world around us be valued over meditating upon creation and all the jewels hidden within? I was well aware that in a month's time I'd be back in the land of traffic jams and rush hours. The week I had to myself in Mozambique awaiting Motshedi's arrival was all the time I needed to fortify a calm inside me that I hoped would outlast the seasons of my mother country.

I spent hours in the morning looking out the window at a sky the color of irises, and writing in my journal. There I described Mozambique's beauty as being like the skeleton of a great warrior. It was like a skeleton, for the country was visibly falling apart. Many of the beautifully arched and curved buildings were in the process of crumbling. Their brightly painted façades were peeling away, to become a kaleidoscope of colors on the sidewalk. When I walked down the streets, it always surprised me that there was a general hum like laughter in the air, and that people weren't walking around with frowns on their faces because of the war that was eating away at their lives and homes. Even the women who sat beneath the trees for hours each day, selling red peppers and peanuts, bubbled with a love for life.

The day Motshedi flew into Mozambique, Mr Rana expressed doubts that her visa had come through. "What do you mean, you hope her visa is ready?" I asked, and in my surprise dropped the spoon with which I had been stirring sugar into my tea. It rang dully against the wooden floor.

"We don't have everything ready yet for her visa, but it is coming. I'm sure it'll be ready by the time she comes this afternoon." Then he walked nonchalantly to the window and remarked about the weather. I was aghast.

"And if it doesn't come through . . .?" I asked carefully.

"She will go back to Botswana then," he said bluntly. "But I'm sure it won't come to that." I began having visions of Motshedi's interrogation by one of the armed guards, a slow, painful torture that would force her into falsely confessing that she was a spy or a refugee.

Luckily, it didn't come to that. Her visa was confirmed by the immigration office and handed to a man standing guard at the airport just as the plane was landing. Motshedi was the third person to come through the airport doors. She wore a bright orange and fuchsia dress that moved like light across her calves. I was so happy to see her that I wound my arm around hers and refused to let go until we got into the car.

There was said to be only one proper grocery store in all of Maputo. This is where Motshedi and I went, the day after her arrival. It was the dollar/rand shop, that imported its food and supplies from abroad. It didn't accept Metical (the national currency), only American dollars and South African rand, which were as good as gold in Mozambique. We passed by many stores on our way to the dollar/rand shop, stores with shelves empty and gray with dust; boxes of plain tea and jars of Vaseline their only wares.

We also passed by vegetable markets, where women stood behind tables selling handmade baskets, tiny silver fish, and colorful spices wrapped in clear plastic. The smell of fish and strong spices always tickled my nose, threatening to make me sneeze and give away my foreignness. Weeks before, a friend had braided my hair into dozens of tiny braids. I didn't know, until I got to Mozambique, that this was how many of the Mozambican women wore their hair. My deep mahogany color already fitted in with the shades of brown and black stirring around me. For once, my tendency to behave like those around me paid off, as I found myself slipping slowly into Mozambique's way of life. I began to feel less like an oddity, and got to a point where I could easily, and with great pity for them being so out of place, point out the few tourists I saw in Mozambique. Their clumsy gaping at Maputo's beauty gave them away even more than their dull safari clothes and sunglasses.

Across the Baia do Espirito Santo, on the outskirts of Maputo's concrete buildings, docks, and rusty fishing boats, lay the small village of Catembe. I first visited its shores a few days before Motshedi's arrival, at a birthday party for a friend of the Ranas. I was excited about crossing the bay, whose waters silently murmured the secrets of the Indian Ocean – a soft gray so distant, it became one with the horizon. Mr Rana pointed to it as we sat in the car, packed tight, surrounded by all the trucks and 4x4s that could fit on the ferry. Where there was standing room, mostly along the side rails where breezes teased scarfed heads, people leaned out over the water, looking out at the shore of Catembe dotted with palm trees.

The village was ancient, as though it had fallen off the vehicle of advancing time years ago; a frozen piece of life that went neither forwards nor backwards. We drove beneath high walls of green foliage, passing brightly painted wooden houses and people walking. Mr Rana stopped the car in front of a house hidden by vines and trees. Inside, the room glowed with the light from a single bare bulb hanging from the ceiling. Each wall was like a chess board of black and white tiles. Mr Rana began pacing up and down the room five minutes after we'd been inside the house. It looked empty. We had come for a party, but where was everybody, not to mention the food? A few moments later, an old Indian man walked into the room from another part of the house. He was wearing a white tee shirt so soaked in sweat that it looked like plastic wrap was holding back his full stomach.

"Welcome, welcome!" he insisted, grabbing all of our hands in his and patting them lightly. He reminded me of those majestic oak trees that live for centuries. A presence about him assumed the respect his age demanded. Even the Ranas' two children, who before had been whimpering about the heat closing in on us like a trap, fell silent when he walked into the room, and offered their hands to him like the rest of us. There was something about old people in Africa that I rarely saw in the States. I saw such grace and pride in them, in a land where the wisdom that comes with age was admired, instead of the arrogance of youth.

While the room filled with people, I kept myself occupied by watching an old western – subtitled in Hindi – on the television in the corner and slapping at mosquitoes, while little girls in pastel dresses filled a table in the center of the room with plates of fried food. There was a fairly large population of Indians in Maputo, and quite a few in Botswana. In both countries, they owned many of the small businesses, as did the British and Americans. In Maputo, it was mainly the Indians and whites I saw driving their own cars, while the blacks were piled to the roof in large run-down buses, or on the back of trucks. It was mainly the Indians and whites I saw in the dollar/rand shop, while mostly blacks thronged the fruit and vegetable markets. There was a tension between these two groups, and I could feel the anger directed toward the Ranas as we drove down the streets in their shiny white car. As I sat in that car, I was conscious of bewildered glances, and, sometimes of looks of that same hate.

Back at the party, a group of men had begun removing Fanta, Coke, and cans of beer from a cooler and fitting them between plates on the table. When they were finished, they stood back to admire their work. The room was now crowded with people, and the heat was stifling. It went quiet; the television was snapped off. Looking around for the first time, I noticed that everyone at the birthday party was Indian except for me. When the silence was just about to grow unbearable, people began to clap, faces erupting in glee. When everyone lunged for a plate of food on the table, someone tapped my shoulder. I turned around. It was a man who looked a few years older than I, wearing a bright floral shirt. He handed me a plate. "You see this?" he asked, pointing to a pot in the middle of the table. It stood like a center-piece, filled with pink mush. I nodded, raising my eyebrows in a feigned delight to eat what he next scooped up and put on my plate. "You want this," he announced, then wormed his way through the crowd to get me a plastic fork. By the time he made his way back to me, he had been slapped on the back a few times, and accepted at least five handshakes. So this was the birthday boy. Handing me the fork, he motioned for me to follow him to the other side of the table. "This is also very good," he smiled, pointing to a plate filled with large prawns. "Hot! Very hot!" he shouted over the noise, waving his hand in front of his open mouth. He watched as I picked up the prawn by its tail and inspected it, its eyes and whiskers still in place. Giving him a weak smile, I nibbled at the pink flesh, stained with red pepper sauce. It burned each part of my mouth it touched. I dabbed at my lips with the edge of a napkin. When I looked back up at him, he was frowning. Looking around the table, he grabbed a grape Fanta. Handing it to me with a triumphant smile, he watched my delight in drinking it. This I could deal with, I thought. I'm sure he was thinking the same thing.

Somehow the village looked different the second time I visited, as Motshedi, Rosalie, Isaac and I ran from the ferry to the man selling tickets, then to the bus, its engine throbbing. Mr Rana told Motshedi and me that one day we'd go with a few others to the village of Catembe. Today was that day. Rosalie and Isaac were members of the Maputo Bahá'í community who decided to join us. We saw them every evening at the national Bahá'í center, when the Bahá'ís gathered to sing and pray. Neither Rosalie nor Issac could speak English, except for a few greetings, and Motshedi and I couldn't speak Portuguese or Ishangane, so we communicated through clumsy gestures and sighs.

Though I felt for Motshedi's plight, as I was in the same position, I enjoyed watching her frustration at not being understood. She was by nature a very extrovert and inquisitive person, and wanted to ask questions about whom we were visiting, where they lived on the island, and how long it took to get there. But she wasn't in her home, Botswana, or even in a predominantly English-speaking country now. In Motshedi's frustration, I glimpsed my own culture shock months before, when I arrived in Africa. Though most of the people in the capital Botswana spoke English, it was as if the rest of the world had been drastically altered. Everything – smells, faces, sounds of disgust, even the constellations in the heavens had become foreign to me. So it must have been even more frustrating for Motshedi, because she was still in Africa, her mother continent, although her world had shifted. She pointed to her wrist where a watch normally went (but which today was inconveniently missing), and asked "How long?" Issac would patiently look at his watch and tell her the time, in carefully enunciated Portuguese numbers. When he saw the perplexed look on her face, he used his fingers to show her the time. But that wasn't what she wanted.

"How do you say 'how long?' in Portuguese?" Motshedi asked me. I looked at her in surprise. It was she who collected Portuguese words, greetings and phrases, in an attempt to learn as much of the language as she could. I'd given up before I'd even started, rationalizing that if I couldn't speak French after studying it for six years in school, I could hardly expect to learn Portuguese in three weeks.

"KT," she said, her voice strained. "Why doesn't he understand what I'm asking him? I ask for the time, then I say 'Bahá'í'. How hard can that be to understand?"

"Very hard, for someone who doesn't speak English," I said, then laughed, loud and unrestrained. Motshedi watched me through narrow eyes until I explained my amusement. "Remember honey, this was your bright idea to go to a place where you didn't speak the language. That's where you are. Mozambique. Welcome to verbal isolation, what I've been experiencing since June."

We were now on the bus, being pushed to one side as more and more people (and chickens) piled in. There were no seats, except for a large black bench stretching full width in the back. All the other chairs had been removed, to make more room. Where the chairs were once nailed down, there were rusty holes in the metal floor. On the side of the bus where we now stood was a large rectangular hole. Its corroded edges were dangerously jagged in some parts. I guessed that this was where a window once was during the bus's better days. As we were shoved even more, Motshedi sat on the frame of the late window. The driver must have noticed her backside sticking out, because he came to the back of the bus and carried on in some language, motioning for her to get up.

The second time he came to the back of the bus, to insist with wild gestures that Motshedi get off, Motshedi sucked her teeth loudly in annoyance and turned back to me.

"Now where were we, KT, before we were so rudely interrupted?"

"Never mind where we were," I answered, "That's the second time that man's come back here asking you to get off that window sill!"

"Actually, we don't know what he's trying to say. He doesn't speak anything I understand," she said, giving me an innocent smile. She shifted on the sill. It groaned and buckled from the weight.

"Motshedi, I don't think he's commenting on your choice of attire." Looking at her wrinkled tee shirt and stained skirt with an air of mock disapproval, she finally gave in with a laugh and

78

got off the window sill. I laughed too, wondering if this was Motshedi's own culture-shocked reaction to life in Mozambique, or just plain stubbornness. Just a few minutes later, Rosalie frantically motioned for us to get off the bus and we began walking up hills of sand, sprinkled with palm trees. As we went further up, the palm trees thinned out. Soon we were high enough to see the village like a green blanket beneath us, and the shimmering bay. It was beautiful. Since Rosalie and Issac were a few steps ahead of us, we had only each other to complain to about the heat that drew sweat, like tears, from our tired bodies.

"They must have known we were coming," I whispered as we rounded the corner of a large house. Under a tree in the back yard, children were dressed in tiny suits, frilly dresses, and shiny black shoes. They looked enviously at our feet, long since liberated from the sandals we held in our hands. We were introduced to a small group of women, then led inside. The first room we entered was cool, with chairs set up in neat rows. Along the walls were pictures of groups of Bahá'ís, a few of the Houses of Worship around the world, the Guardian and 'Abdu'l-Bahá. In the front were three chairs; one for me, from which I spoke on the Covenant, one for Motshedi, as she translated what I said into Setswana and later spoke herself on the life and station of Bahá'u'lláh, the third for a woman from Botswana who translated Motshedi's Setswana into one of the indigenous languages of Catembe.

The talks were very short – even allowing for the translations – just a few minutes on each subject. When we asked the audience if they had any questions, we were met with silence. Then a harsh whispering could be heard coming from the back of the room where some of the older folk were sitting. Ten little children were nudged to the front of the room. Uncertainly, they lined up in front of us. They began to sing, their feet tapping the wooden floor. Motshedi gave a big "whoopee!" and joined them, twirling and singing and laughing. Wherever I went in Africa, song and dance seemed to be one of the surest gateways to the heart. It meant so much more than just sitting and listening to a speaker drone on. When you truly love something, you want to love it with your body, heart and soul, not just your intellect. The songs they sang were about Bahá'u'lláh and their joy at being Bahá'ís. They were songs telling of love that stirred the soul.

"Mozambique is dying, friends!" Margaret told us at the Bahá'í center the next Sunday. She aimed her outrage, and tightly balled fist– its veins visibly intertwined and swirling like an uprooted tree – at no one in particular, but we each felt it directed toward ourselves.

"Dying!" Margaret repeated. "Where's Chris?" she asked, eyes darting about. He had slipped outside to fetch his little girl, who had wandered into the street. Someone told Margaret this, and she said, "Well he can't very well translate while he's standing out there, can he now?" and with a mighty "humpf!" her face and body sank into a frown. For a minute, we all looked out the tall narrow door through which Chris and his daughter had disappeared. They came back into the center, Chris apologizing and holding his daughter, who still clutched a flower from outside in her tiny hand. Margaret continued.

"Mozambique is dying, and what are we doing about it? Sitting comfortably on our butts in Maputo." Chris rendered her words into Portuguese as Margaret looked down at the tiled floor. When Chris finished, she concluded in a hoarse and tired voice, "We have to do something about it, friends."

I loved Margaret from the moment Mrs Rana told me about the "American pioneer." Just talking about her had brought a smile to her face, and light to her eyes. "Yes . . ." Veena Rana said while pouring me another cup of tea, "you will love Margaret. You will see. We all love her. She is so . . ." her eyes scanned the room for the correct word, then she said, ". . . so alive." Seeing her in the Bahá'í center proved just how right Veena was. Margaret's spirit filled the tiny room with such energy!

During a lapse in the conversation that evening at the Bahá'í center, Mr Rana had asked Margaret to tell everyone about the conference in Swaziland she had just returned from. That's what started her recounting statistics and casualties of the ongoing civil war in Mozambique, that sent my heart in a frenzy. What was I doing here?

"Friends," Margaret began again, "I didn't realize the seriousness of the war until I left Mozambique and read about it in an international newspaper in Swaziland. It was there that I read all those statistics I just told you about." Everyone was looking down, unable to look her in the eye as she explained the article.

"The article ends with this line: 'Will somebody please end this damn war?'" There was a slight pause before Chris translated her last sentence. He had to take a breath of air before beginning, and even then the words were slow in coming. After his translation was completed, he bowed his head like the rest of us.

It was Margaret's idea to hold a "Prayer for Peace Rally", in which we should invite the whole neighborhood to join. An hour later, we had split into four groups of two. Margaret's job was done. We had been properly inspired, and now we were to invite the neighbors. Margaret sat in a corner, watching us go out, excited and eager to teach. We all decided she should stay inside the cool center and rest. The apartments around the neighborhood were many storeys high, and would require a lot of climbing, and Margaret, who was 80 (or thereabouts) didn't need that kind of work.

Rosalie, Chris's wife, was my partner. We all had a few pamphlets with (in two languages) the Báb's prayer:

Is there any Remover of difficulties save God? Say: Praised be God! He is God! All are His servants, and all abide by His bidding.

We were going to pass these out to people and ask that they read them as a prayer for peace and for the solution of personal problems. Most people let us into their homes, and brought us cool drinks before they even knew who we were. I watched their faces light up as Rosalie told them why we were there. Though I couldn't understand what was being said, I could tell that everyone Rosalie spoke to liked what she was saying.

The "Prayer for Peace Rally" was held the next day. Motshedi and I were asked to say something short about how

Bahá'ís view peace, as an introduction for the prayers to follow. Thirty-two people arrived that evening. Chairs were already set up in one of the large rooms of the center. Though the window sills and trims were in place, there was no glass. Cool breezes blew in slender green palm leaves from outside throughout the night.

When it was time for me to speak, I spoke first of the suffering going on all around the world, starting with racism in America. The audience could understand that, as prejudice is universal. Then I told them something that 'Abdu'l-Bahá said in Paris Talks, about war being the lowest deed:men fighting for the very earth that will eventually be their grave. Even animals have better reasons to fight, and to die. Everyone knows that nothing is gained by fighting. What the Bahá'ís are trying to do, I explained, is to help bring about the world peace God has promised us. Not an easy task, but this is our job on earth.

When I finished speaking, Motshedi stood up and outlined the steps which the Bahá'í teachings state are needed to bring world peace. She especially stressed the need for a universal auxiliary language. She realized this principle having come to Mozambique, she said, where she was still in Africa, yet at the same time a foreigner.

Chris rose, and asked that people say prayers for peace. People of various religious backgrounds stood up one by one, and prayed aloud. When all the prayers had been said, the silent room was filled with the warm spirit of love and unity. I looked around at all the beautiful faces, in awe of what could bring so many perfect strangers together for the purpose of a peaceful world.

Quietly, people began to rise and speak before the group. An old man was the first. He rose slowly and spoke softly. Chris whispered a translation of what the old man was saying. "Many years ago," he said, "there was an Indian merchant living in this house." The old man looked around at the walls and ceiling of the Bahá'í center, as if remembering. "Then he moved away. We heard that the house would again be occupied. We didn't know by whom, and we could only hope for the best. We saw the sign "Bahá'í" over the door, and could only guess what that meant: "Bahá'í." He paused, his face thoughtful, before continuing. "It fills me with such joy to now know what Bahá'ís are: people working toward peace in a world with so many of those who want to promote war." He placed his hand over his heart and stood like that for a long time before sitting down. Other people spoke and gave their views of a peaceful world, but my thoughts stayed on what the old man had said.

It was slow moving down the dirt road winding through Matola. We had turned off the main paved road, leaving the last glimpses of Maputo behind. Matola was only ten kilometres outside Maputo, but I still felt nervousness rise like a madness in my chest. Only inside Maputo were we relatively safe. Outside the city limits we were open prey for anything. I thought of Veena Rana's stories of what happened outside the major cities, and wondered what she was thinking, as she sat in the front of the car. We were driving slower now. The road was scattered with people in silver and turquoise wheelchairs. Their pants from the knee down swung with a horrid emptiness.

We were driving slowly enough to see the sweat shine on their faces as their strong arms maneuvered the wheelchairs over rocks and bumps. We came to a section of the village where green, open-sided tents stood either side of the road. Mr Rana's voice came flat from the front of the car, telling us that those in the tents were casualties of war. I looked again. There were so many dark, still figures lying on those beds, their truncated limbs visible from the car. Slowly, I was beginning to understand the consequences of Mozambique's civil war. Margaret's rage, and the old man's words at the peace rally, began to have a whole new meaning to me.

Ethel stood up on her porch to greet us as we parked in front of her house. A deep fuchsia color, the house sat where the road ended and forked to either side. Ethel and her sons were members of the Matola Bahá'í community. Other members of the community drifted in as the evening passed into night. We had already each said prayers in our own mother tongue, when Ethel began talking, with Mr Rana translating. He started off in a low voice, as if afraid that his breath might blow out the flame of the lantern on the table before him.

"A few hours ago, she says, she decided to go visit some friends in the next village. She was all prepared to go, standing on the porch, when her legs refused to work." I looked over at Ethel who was nodding slowly at Motshedi and me, rubbing her legs gently. A flicker of a smile crossed her lips, and then like a shadow cast by the lantern's dancing flame, it disappeared. She began to speak again, then turned to watch our faces as Mr Rana told us what she said.

She called her son, and he said, "Don't go to that village. The bandits have killed some people there yesterday and even today. Stay here and read prayer number 40.* I think you will have visitors soon." She went back to her house and read prayer number 40 from her prayer book." Then she began to straighten up the house for visitors. When all the straightening was done, she sat on the porch to wait. And here we are!" We talked for a long time about how the Bahá'ís could help bring about peace in Mozambique, by healing hearts through the teachings of love and unity. After speaking of the success of Maputo's "Prayer for Peace Rally," Ethel and the other Bahá'ís of the Matola community decided that they too would hold one of their own. There wasn't much more they could do in a village so plagued with the pain and suffering of war.

Pemba, a village in northern Mozambique, was our next stop, according to the teaching plan laid out by the National Spiritual Assembly of Mozambique. Everyone had heard the hushed tales of war in the North. Since government troops were concentrated on the capital city in the South, the North was almost isolated.

Inside the plane, rows of people sat fanning themselves with newspapers. On the walls were the gray outline figures of fish, alligators and tigers, like drawings from a coloring book waiting to be filled in. Hendric and Thelonius sat in the row behind Motshedi and me. They were two youth from Maputo who were

* In books of Bahá'í prayers, prayers are often numbered for ease of reference. The numbers do not form part of the text, and are of no significance.

joining us for the teaching trip to the North. Thelonius was known as the musician of the Maputo Bahá'í community.

When the Ranas first brought me to the Bahá'í center, Thelonius sang and played a song on his guitar which was written especially for the occasion. The only word I had recognized was my name, Kemba. Hendric was a young member of the National Spiritual Assembly of Mozambique, and seemed older than his years. Maybe this was because he had been physically changed by the war. While still a young boy, he had stepped on a landmine, which had left him with one useless leg.

As we lifted off the ground with a great shudder, I looked down on the thin wispy roads cutting through the countryside below. We flew low enough to see that they were quite empty. I'd heard that the roads from village to village and city to city were blocked by bandits, who would shoot anyone trying to drive through. These attacks were reported on the radio as regularly as the weather. For miles and miles I searched for cars and trucks on the road, but saw not a single one. The emptiness made it look like a dark river. Then we were really over water. Motshedi rattled on about spits and long shore drifts and other geographical features she'd long ago learned about in school, that she could see now in the ocean below us. By the time Motshedi stopped for a quick nap, the world below us looked like a pointillist drawing, its subject a little out of focus.

For some time we'd been sitting on the dusty sidewalk, on top of a hill, from which we could see the red and green coast of Pemba, and the village sticking out like a thumb into the perfect blue ocean.

"Here comes Hendric", Motshedi said (between second and third ballet position). I looked up from a book I was reading on Zen to acknowledge Hendric walking toward us, with another man. I dove back into my reading. Thelonius had been singing slow melodious songs on the guitar, but now began putting it back in its plastic bag. Motshedi moved from third position to fourth, unaware of the strange looks she attracted, practicing her ballet positions in the middle of town. "Did you find a place for us to stay?" she called. Hendric nodded. He had left over an hour before, in search of Bahá'ís, or hotels with rooms for us to stay one week in Pemba. When the two men approached us, we were introduced to Mr Mputhanga, a Bahá'í of many years experience who was more than happy to introduce Motshedi and me to the "real Mozambique" by allowing us to stay with him for one night. Mr Mputhanga taught English at a large secondary school whose grounds we passed through, as we went from one side of Pemba to the other. The stores and tiled houses were separated from the village by two large school buildings standing in a field.

"This is our suburbs, see?" Mr Mputhanga smiled proudly over his shoulder, before returning his gaze to the rugged path before him. The paths were wide and stony, winding between bamboo skeleton homes.

"Why can't I imagine two dogs and a station wagon?" Motshedi muttered under her breath. Some of the homes were still in the process of being built, and I could see where rocks were stuffed into empty cavities between parallel bamboo frames. Then a reddish paste, the color of the earth, was caked over the walls. The village wasn't set up like those I'd seen in Botswana. Here these rectangular homes were laid out like houses in the big city, with a large path, wide as a road, running between them.

By now, it was dusk. Light from fires and lanterns had dotted our walk. To get to Mr Mputhanga's home, we had to cut through a neighbor's yard. We closed the gate, and were greeted by the glare of a fluorescent light, buzzing from his front porch. It cast a deep green hue over our skin. We were looking at three children laying on the ground, draped in colorful fabrics, when Mr Mputhanga came out from the house, first with chairs, then with bowls of hot food. He saw the look of surprise I gave Motshedi as he served us rice and stew on shiny white plates. It was the first time during my six-month stay with families all over Southern Africa that I had been served by a male member of the household. "My wife, she's out with friends," he explained before going back into the house for water.

The night was kind and warm. We sat outside for hours after we'd finished eating. The bugs didn't bother us, drawn to the fluorescent light behind Mr Mputhanga, the glare obscuring his face. He told us he was building a much bigger, grander house. This one just wasn't big enough. He looked back at his house with a look of disgust, then pointed toward the answer to his problems. Over in one corner of the yard sat a small metal and wood device for molding bricks. The bricks could only be made one at a time, and each one took a whole day to dry.

"I start my house at two thousand bricks," he whispered, aware of the sleeping children at our side. Looking down at them, he said, "They like to sleep outside beneath the stars." We all looked up. A thousand stars shone through a black night. A few minutes later he showed us to our room and handed us a well-used Michael Jackson tape to put in the cassette player, on a chair near the door.

After our night in Mr Mputhanga's house, we were accommodated in an apartment in town. Motshedi and I slept in the room of two brothers, who in turn slept on bags of rice in the pantry. Everyone had been introduced to me, except for a short man who fixed delicious fish stews and soups from a Bunsen burner stove in the kitchen. He also brought up fresh buckets of water each morning from the well near the base of the stairs, so we could wash in the bath tub. There was no running water in the apartment. I never found out whether this was because the water lines were cut, or because the plumbing was defunct.

Once I smiled at the little man. I assumed that he was the little brother whose job it was to do all the housework and cooking. He was plucking feathers from a freshly soaked chicken in the kitchen, and averted his eyes as if embarrassed. A few moments later he looked up and smiled nervously, as if afraid that someone would see him. When my greetings to the little man became a regular occurrence, I was taken aside by one of the brothers and told that he was a houseboy. He didn't have to tell me that this meant that he was to be treated like the hired help he was. Later on, it was explained to me that, unlike countries in Southern Africa where maids were the norm and part of the "welfare system" of society, northern Mozambique was more East African in its culture. It was an East African custom to have houseboys instead of maids, because men were considered the more responsible sex.

Mr Mputhanga eventually found us a ride to Miese, a village thirty kilometres outside Pemba. There were only a handful of cars in Pemba, and he must have enquired of all his contacts before finding one willing to take us that far out. And Mr Mputhanga did have his contacts. Being the English teacher of the village, he was highly regarded by all, including his former students. We kept running into them when Mr Mputhanga took Motshedi and me on walks around town. It didn't take long for us to realize that as long as we dressed in beautiful fabrics like the women around us, and we didn't open our mouths, we went unnoticed. It was a trick we used well, because when Mr Mputhanga, whom we'd nicknamed "The Big Man of Pemba," paraded us around town, it took people a long time to guess where we were from. Up and down the streets of Pemba he would display us. When we asked him where we were going, he'd answer that he was "showing us life in northern Mozambique". Whenever we approached someone Mr Mputhanga knew, which was just about every person who walked by, they'd stop and greet one another, making small talk. The men he stopped to talk to were always keenly aware of our presence. Mr Mputhanga held their curiosity like a heart, frantically beating in the palm of his hand. Instead of introducing us, he'd let the curiosity build.

"And how is your father?" Mr Mputhanga would ask casually after initial greetings were over.

"My father is doing well, quite well," the other man would answer, peeking over Mr Mputhanga's shoulder at Motshedi and me, as we rolled our eyes and sighed. Mr Mputhanga was at it again.

"And how is your uncle? Your brother-in-law?"

"Yes, yes, they are both doing quite well. Same as my father. Quite well."

"That is very good," Mr Mputhanga would say, his lips like a prune as he watched boys playing with tires in the street. It would be a long time until either man spoke again, Mr Mputhanga's friend looking helplessly toward Motshedi and me, Mr Mputhanga acting as if he'd forgotten we were there.

"Okay," Mr Mputhanga would finally say, clapping his hands together as if preparing some great announcement. "Now brother, here I have two visitors for you to meet." The other man would laugh, relieved and happy that Mr Mputhanga had at last decided to honor him with an introduction to his mysterious visitors.

"This here, my man, is Motshedi." Both men nodded in her direction. "And Motshedi's from . . . guess where?" There followed a listing of the major cities of Mozambique. Mr Mputhanga would stand aside shaking his head at each of the man's guesses until he could do nothing but stand bewildered, shaking his head and staring at Motshedi.

"Brother, you are wrong," Mr Mputhanga would say with a laugh. "Guess where this Motshedi from? Bechuanaland!"*

This news would send the other man into hysterics. "No, brother! Bechuanaland, another African country? Ah, man, so far!"

Mr Mputhanga would nod calmly to himself, waiting till his friend's excitement died down. Then he'd point to me and put the same question.

"I know an African sister when I see one!" the man would say, looking at my tiny jagged braids. "She is definitely from either this place or another African country around here." Then he'd run through a list of the surrounding villages and towns, then neighbouring countries, until he stood flustered, scratching his head.

"No, brother, you are wrong *again!*" Mr Mputhanga would laugh. "Kemba is not from another African country or even Mozambique. Kemba is from – America!"

"No, not America!" his friend would shout. "Why you want tell me such a joke in this heat, man? Why you want to tell me such things? I can tell a Mozambique sister! I may be old, my friend, but I am not yet blind. She is definitely an African sister. My heart is too weak to take this news, too weak I tell you, man!"

It was at this point that Mr Mputhanga would give me my cue. A nod of his head was my signal to speak, putting his friend out of his misery. One word from my mouth could convince anyone that I was indeed from America.

---

* From 1885 until independence in 1966, Botswana was a British protectorate, and went by the name, "Bechuanaland".

"Yes, I am from America," I would say to the man who stood shcoked, staring at me in amazement.

And both Kemba and Motshedi will be here for one week to tell everybody about the Bahá'í Faith around eight at Paulina's. Both Kemba and Motshedi are Bahá'ís.' You could see the man trying to remember if he was free any nights this week. "We must go now. We have many things to get done." With that, we'd walk down the road a ways until we came across more of Mputhanga's friends and enacted the same introduction. In this way, we were introduced to Pemba, and Pemba was introduced to us. And every evening, around eight o'clock, ten or fifteen of Mr Mputhanga's friends would show up at Paulina's.

At these meetings, Motshedi and I let Hendric and Thelonius do most of the talking, for two reasons. The first reason had to do with language. If you can speak someone's mother tongue, an advantage Thelonius and Hendric had over us, you can speak to their heart. The other reason was just common sense. Motshedi and I were the strangers in this country. Thelonius and Hendric were just north of their home town, but they were still from Mozambique. They knew what their countrymen wanted to hear, what they needed to hear, and what they should hear. If I were to speak, it would be from an American Bahá'í perspective, on the world and on the Faith, which may well have been irrelevant to the people we wanted to teach. But if I were ever assailed by any feelings of being redundant, as sometimes happened, I'd think of what I'd learned on earlier parts of my African teaching trips: that if progress is to be made, then every individual must find, and fulfill, their own unique role in any given situation. Here in Mozambique, my role, as I understood it, was to be a living example of the Bahá'í world community, a catalyst to further action by the Mozambique Bahá'í community. So I always sat silent at these evening meetings, swallowing my pride when it got too big, and singing songs in my head as everyone spoke in languages unknown to me.

*

The village of Miese was on top of a hill, just off a gnarled dirt road that twisted so much, we didn't see the man until we were nearly on top of him. He stood still and was not about to move, even though the driver beeped several times and spat out words that I knew weren't friendly as we wove around him. When we approached a clearing a few yards away, we could see the village clearly. We could also see the villagers all standing straight, like the man in the middle of the road, saluting a red flag with yellow symbols, which was being raised on a wooden pole. The soldier who raised the flag clicked his heels when his task was done, and walked to a hut a few feet away. As the villagers began the routine of daily life again, a man scurried up to Mr Mputhanga. They spoke to one another with the excitement of old friends reunited, and we were led to a bench in the shade, and told to wait.

A man sitting across from me was carving a profile onto a piece of ebony. He was working on the curves of the ear when another man came up and whispered to Mr Mputhanga's friend, who in turn whispered to Mr Mputhanga. His face fell for the second time when he told us that the only place that could be arranged for us to speak was in the main party headquarters.

Inside the main party headquarters, there was a wooden stage with chairs, and a large table. The rest of the room was half filled with people sitting on the dirt floor. Two old men sat in the front in mismatched suits, bright blue flip-flops on their feet.

"Should we start now?" I asked Mr Mputhanga. He was sitting on the edge of his seat, looking around nervously. I had to call his name several times before he heard me.

"No, no, not yet." He strained to look out into the empty village. "Not yet. We have more people to come." His voice sounded weak. We waited. Suddenly Mr Mputhanga's twitching stopped. A hush fell over the crowd. I looked out past the walls which were only half built. A procession of men was coming toward us, in formation like birds flying South. My eyes fell down their dull green uniformed bodies to the long German rifles in their hands. They walked into the room and looked around. With a grunt, one of the men leaned his rifle against the

91

wall, butt end down, and slung his hat over the barrel. The other men did the same and sat down beside the old men in flip-flops.

"Now we can begin," Mr Mputhanga whispered. One of the uniformed men stood up, introduced a handful of those present, and sat down again. "Now the chief has come and introduced the important people." Mr Mputhanga whispered before standing up and introducing Motshedi, Hendric, Thelonius and me. Motshedi and I spoke about the importance of peace, and some of the steps necessary to gain it. Hendric and Thelonius spoke about other aspects of the Bahá'í Faith.

After twenty minutes or so, I began to study the faces of those in the audience. I watched one of the old men in flip-flops listen for a moment to Hendric, turn to his friend and speak loudly, then listen to Hendric again. His voice was loud and irritating. I looked around. Nobody else seemed to mind. Mr Mputhanga leaned over and explained that the two men were the village preachers. One of them didn't understand what was being said, the other was explaining it to him.

When the talk was over, I handed out pamphlets. Some held them upside down in their hands, squinting over the words, as if deciphering code. Someone asked how to become a Bahá'í, so Mr Mputhanga asked how many people wanted to become Bahá'ís. Slowly, hands were raised. The preachers were the first to raise their hands, and the chief among the last.

The man who had been working on the ebony carving when we first arrived stood up and proudly handed the figure to Mr Mputhanga. He pointed to the bottom where he had written his own name and the name of the village. Mr Mputhanga handed the carving to Motshedi, muttering that it should go to the ladies, and Motshedi turned right around and handed it to me. "It should go to the one who is going the farthest away," she said.

We were supposed to fly out of Pemba to Maputo on the 28th of the month. On the 30th, Motshedi and I had tickets from Maputo to Johannesburg to Capetown. We caught a ride to the airport in Pemba early in the afternoon, and waited all day. Around eight o'clock a man strolled into the lobby where everyone sat waiting, and made an announcement. Everyone got up and walked out of the airport.

"What's going on?" Motshedi asked Hendric. He just shook his head and went to catch us a lift back to Paulina's apartment. Motshedi and I had a string of planes to catch in the next few days, and our schedule didn't permit delays. The last thing we could afford was a day's hold up. On the ride back to the apartment, we pried Hendric for information about the delayed plane. He looked embarrassed while telling us that the plane had a flat tire, and somebody had been sent to fly back to Maputo to get a spare.

"Hero" Thelonius wrote on a scrap of paper back at Paulina's apartment. Then he slowly asked, "Who – is – our – hero?"

"It's me," Hendric shouted as he limped to a seat on the patio. Thelonius shook his head and grinned. He was enjoying himself. I asked him if it was me, and he shook his head again. "Bahá'u'lláh!" he said over his shoulder before disappearing onto the patio. I turned over in my mind the reasons Bahá'u'lláh would have us wait in the hot airport for so long, when we wouldn't be able to fly out of Pemba. I could think of several, starting with the stories I'd heard about planes being shot down by ground-to-air missiles. I eventually fell asleep to the monotonous sound of Motshedi asking the name of every object in the room in Portuguese, accompanied by Hendric's laughter, a sound like the cracking of nut shells.

To watch the African sky

We parted at a small dusty bus station in South Africa. Motshedi was headed for Jwaneng, where her family awaited her safe return from Mozambique, while I was headed further north to Gaborone. I had a few days to pack and say my good-byes before a plane whisked me off the continent. My bus was scheduled to leave before Motshedi's, so she sat with me, while her own bus finished loading.

"Well, honey, I guess this is it, as they say," Motshedi said, feigning happiness. I rapped my nails against the plastic seat in front of me and tried to smile. "Now KT," she sighed, "you know you've no business being sad."

"No business?" I asked.

"Yes Kemba, no business at all." Motshedi took my hand and we both looked out at the busy station, at the buses loading and unloading. "It's a small world," she said in a voice so weak I could hardly make out the words. "It's a small world."

"Are you referring to our 'plan of action'?" I asked. Motshedi nodded and grinned. Several weeks before, when we realized our time together was running out, we devised a plan to meet halfway between Southern Africa and America in a year's time. We would organize a teaching trip in England and then beg our parents to allow us to go. Nearly eight months away from home had done little to dim the memory of my parents' strictness; I had little hope that they would allow another transatlantic journey, even if it was in the interests of the Faith, but pride kept me from sharing these thoughts with Motshedi.

The bus to Jwaneng revved its engines, with a jarring scream and a cloud of smoke. Motshedi stood up and gave me one last hug. Her face buried in the folds of my jacket, she whispered,

"No tears allowed," and with a smile, she walked off the bus and into the chaos of the station. I watched her until her swaying figure was lost in the crowd.

Hugging Ed, Corey, and Helen goodbye at Gaborone airport a few days later, I felt just the same as if I were going to Mozambique for a month or two. I think they were confused by my rush to enter the departure gates and be on my journey.

"Just one more picture, Kemba. Right here by the gates," Ed said, pushing me lightly towards the others who were already grouped together. Then, as if I might not have been aware of it myself, he added, "You do know you're leaving Africa, don't you?" With upraised eyebrows he laughed, and snapped the picture.

I did not feel the sadness work its way through me until the tiny Air Botswana craft lifted off the ground, and I took one last look at the hills on the horizon, dulled by distance. By the time I tried to breathe in their beauty, they were too far away.

After my third month in Africa I stopped taking pictures of strangers. I'd tired of viewing Africa, her people and places, as a perpetual photo opportunity. The feeling I hoped to emerge from Africa with was one of harmony with a people and a culture I had once, long before my birth, been a part of; not further proof of the alienation against which I, as a black American, was already struggling. Pictures of startled villagers and sagging rondavaals did little, I felt, to lessen the ever widening gap between "them" and "us". I'll never forget the look of humiliation in Mrs Mputanga's eyes one morning as Motshedi and I toted our cameras to her toilet – the likes of which we'd never seen before – to show the folks back home how people answered the call of nature in the villages of northern Mozambique. It was the same look of humiliation and alienation I often saw in the faces of those who, in the villages, cities and townships, were bombarded by the flipping camera shutters of people who had never extended a hand of friendship or even asked their names, let alone permission to walk away with their image. Secretly, unable to rationalize my feelings to others, I resolved never to be the cause of that kind of humiliation again.

Africa had the collective effect of rounding off my sharp Western edges. Reluctance to capture my surroundings on photographic paper was just one example of the changes I began to notice in myself. Another was my newly acquired taste in food. Whereas before, I had been finicky to the point of obsession, I left Africa with a willingness to eat whatever was placed before me. Mere months before, just the smell of potatoes would be enough to make my stomach turn over. After a few weeks in Africa, denied the choice I'd so taken for granted in the States, potatoes became my favourite starch. I began to have frequent and vivid dreams about the white root I had previously shunned, as the taste of food withered in importance to its mere availability.

It was easy to convince my parents to allow me a few days in England on my way back home. They knew I had English friends from the STAR project, and confidently arranged my five day stopover. But when the five days drew to a close and I requested a longer stay, their confidence waned, fueling the fear that their daughter no longer wanted to come home. Hundreds of miles away, they pondered how they had offered their daughter as a gift to the world beyond the suburbs and comforts of middle class America – a gift that had been readily accepted. What was their promise of home and security in comparison to the world, and its hidden gems, awaiting my discovery?

In Gaborone, Uncle Louie and Auntie Sylvia had to sweet talk the airport officials into allowing me aboard with my five bags. After the officials were convinced that I was a good American girl who meant no harm by this blatant disregard for airport regulations, I was given permission to board. I regretted my cumbersome belongings later, as I pulled and yanked my trolley around London Heathrow airport in search of the underground station and its left luggage office. Heather had known she would be unable to pick me up from the airport, so she'd given careful directions to guide my movements from the time I dropped off most of my bags at left luggage, though the London Underground, until I boarded a train from central London to Sheffield.

It was thrilling to travel on the Underground, packed in with commuters and students and foreign tourists, everyone's eyes afraid to meet those of their neighbors. I tried to carry myself with whimsical detachment, but my curiosity was too strong. How strange it was to be surrounded by hundreds of white faces, when, just a few hours before, I had been surrounded by hundreds of black faces. I found it impossible not to sneak glances at this segment of humanity, whose faces seemed pallid and who seemed so thoroughly bound up, physically and emotionally, that I wondered if they were ashamed of those parts of themselves that might have shown.

I hardly recognized Heather as she jumped from the car to greet me at the station. She looked different without the backdrop of Botswana's desert and sun. I strained to remember conversations we'd had, adventures we'd shared, desperate to confirm that this was the same woman.

In Botswana, Heather had been vibrant and colorful, but here she seemed withdrawn and pale. I told her this when we arrived at her flat, where she led me to her upstairs bedroom. Turning on the light, I saw that the walls were covered with photographs of men and women from the villages Heather had visited, and of the friends she had made. In one corner was a weaving of a village scene she had bravely haggled down to a reasonable price at the Botswana Trades Fair. She'd made her room a tribute to Africa. Flipping through pictures, we spoke of the people and the places that had flavored our stay. Looking back, even painful memories warmed with the glow of recollection:the teaching trip to the desert when we almost ran out of food and water and were reduced to eating a rabbit, freshly killed on the road, my naïve attempts to leave Botswana without proof of my residency, and the slow, inevitable departure of the youth service volunteers from Botswana to their respective homes.

That night I dreamt of Africa. I awoke startled by what I first thought was a group of Africans smiling down at me, only to realize that they were just the pictures on Heather's walls.

I met Hoda at a Bahá'í Societies conference in Manchester that we attended the following day. He was just one of the many conference participants who were interested in the unfamiliar:

namely, Africa in pictures, which I carried around in a small plastic bag. I promised to show them to him within an hour, and, when the allotted time had passed while I sat with Erfan reminiscing about Botshabelo, Hoda came to find me.

It wasn't easy to pull us from our conversation, for I then sought the company of those who reminded me of the continent I was painfully missing. But Hoda's determination to learn about Africa was stronger than mine. He soon succeeded in prying me away, and sat with me in a quiet corner of the hall. As I went through the photographs, explaining each scene and face, sometimes launching into a story that a photograph precipitated, Hoda sat entranced: these were the places he wanted to pioneer to, the experiences he longed for. His earnest desire to learn about a place to which he'd never been heartened me, partly because it was so different from the responses I had encountered thus far. There were many who wanted to see photographs and hear stories that would confirm their own stereotypical image of Africa. There were those who had wanted to see photographs of lions and elephants and zebras, pygmies and warriors and chiefs. But Hoda was different. He impressed me because he wasn't interested in the Africa of films and novels, but in the Africa I had seen, felt, and traveled, and which I was all too willing to share.

It came as no surprise then that when I had to phone my parents a few days later to request a longer stay, Hoda offered the only solution my parents could accept. It was by no means an easy conversation. "Kemba, is that you?," Dad asked when he picked up the phone and heard the static.

"Yes, this is – "

"Hey everybody, Kemba is on the phone from England! Come quick, she ain't got all day to wait for y'all!"

"Hi everybody!"

"Hi! How's England?"

"It's gr – "

"When are you coming home?"

"Um, that's what I wanted to talk to you about."

Silence.

"What? I know you're not thinking of staying?!"

"Well, I've met lots of people here, and you know I have

quite a few friends from Botswana I haven't seen for a while. . . .
I was hoping I could stay longer than just five days."

"You must be out of your mind! Absolutely not."

Outside the phone box, Hoda was grinning and nodding. I
shook my head and frowned.

"Honey, what would you do in England?" Mom asked in a
voice made gentle by worry.

"Well, there are lots of friends I could visit. . . . I could spend
more time with them."

"Doing what?"

"Traveling around. Visiting and catching up."

More silence. I could tell they weren't going for the gypsy
idea.

"But Kemba, we thought you missed us! We thought you
wanted to come home!" I started to feel choked up. Of course I
missed them. I had been gone for eight months, but I was also
having the time of my life! Ulysses had taken nineteen years to
return home. I was only asking for a two week extension.

"Honey, why don't you call us back tomorrow. We'll have
this all figured out by then."

Weeks later I was to learn that at this point Ali repaid me for
years of sneaking him candy bars when he should have been
watching his weight. A few hours after our phone conversation,
he sat our parents down and gave them a talking to. Ali reminded them that I had been serving the Faith for eight months in
Southern Africa. He reminded them of the trials and hardships
I'd had to endure traveling through a desert, with little money
and little food.

"Don't you think that after all this she deserves two weeks of
fun in England with her friends?" Ali's words must have hit
home. When I phoned the next day, my parents told me I could
stay longer.

"But only on one condition," my Dad said. "I want you to
stay with a Bahá'í family, not with your buddies."

"No problem," Hoda said when I told him and the other
STAR youth of my parent's decision. "I just happen to be going
up to Scotland for a week to visit my parents. Why don't you
come with me? We might even be able to arrange for you to
speak to some of our friends about Africa."

99

My trip to Scotland and my stay with Hoda and his family was a period of calm, like I had not experienced since my first week alone in Mozambique. Now, when I no longer had to worry about catching the next plane or finding the next meal, tiredness descended upon me like night. Suddenly, with enough distance between me and Africa to be able to see her clearly, feelings I had unknowingly suppressed began to seep slowly and painfully to the surface. While Hoda drew out more and more African stories from me, he also, quite unintentionally, drew out the glamorless and mundane.

I remember quite well the place where I first confided in him. We were staying with friends in Newcastle upon Tyne on our way up to Scotland. Hoda had asked about the treatment of women in Botswana. Previous responses from former youth service volunteers had implied that the men of Botswana often had a lot to learn about the equality of the sexes. Was that how I saw it? Quite often, I confided, while walking down the streets of Gaborone either alone or with a girlfriend, a passing man would reach out and grab me, refusing to let go until he was shouted off, or his hand was pushed away. I further explained that this never bothered me as much as it did the other female volunteers who were sometimes upset to the point of tears, and who would then refuse to walk any distance without male escorts.

I paused here. I wasn't sure how to end this story, or if I had answered his question, so I sat for some time moving my lips in a pantomime of speech. Hoda, sitting a respectable distance from my lounge chair, mistook my pantomime for softly spoken words, sat up suddenly and leaned in my direction. What happened next frightened both of us. Hoda's sudden movement, even though we were separated by the length of the room, alarmed me. I jumped away, terrified, from Hoda's side of the room then froze in my tension. Hoda slowly sank back into his seat in an attempt to pacify me. It was then that we both realized that I was much more affected by certain negative experiences than I was willing to admit. My response to Hoda's movement was not unfamiliar. I had seen the same responses before when strange men had lunged towards my female friends in Botswana. It was a mixture of fear and dismay, and I thought

100

the day would never come when I would respond in the same manner.

So began a period of unwinding. To the surprise of both of us, there were other emotions from other experiences that came slowly to the forefront. Sometimes it was a smell that reminded me of the chips we used to eat walking through dusty Maun, or an overheard comment that would bring back the discussion about the all-black Thanksgiving Day, or a facial expression which would remind me of Mrs Semela as we waited for a combi to Bloemfontein. There seemed to be no rhyme or reason to this montage. I often felt as though I were a storm of recollections, serving no purpose but cleansing away the remains of one journey, making me ready to begin another. But then there emerged an eye in the storm: the thing around which it all was centered, where at last there was calm. And in this center two things were bound inextricably together, much as they had been all along: the process of discovery and rediscovery of what it meant, to others and to myself, to be a Bahá'í, and to be black.

Corey had once told me that, after being in Africa for only a few weeks, when he looked in the mirror he was always shocked to see his white face staring back at him. In a way, that summed up my own initial conception of color. Growing up in virtually all-white suburbs, I had, without realizing it, been shocked every day of my life to look into the mirror and see what was reflected back at me. The decision to serve in Africa arose partly from an unconscious desire to right that wrong. By being surrounded by hundreds thousands of people that shared my features and color I felt it acceptable to look the way I did. The standards of normality had switched, and I was at last on the "right" side. My confidence in myself soared. But then came the realization that the issue of color wasn't as simple as black and white. It, too, had all kinds of nuances and shades. The incident of the Thanksgiving celebration, my observations, discussions with others, made me realize that it's not only black people who are seeking belonging; we all are in our own way.

Only from witnessing and learning to appreciate a fuller extent of the world's diversity, did I come to appreciate that

that standard Bahá'í motto, "unity in diversity", meant I could no longer allow myself to be comfortable with all-white, all-black, all-*anything* – but only a potpourri of humanity that was richly colored.

Diversity included playing a variety of roles. In Africa we soon learned that our reputations as "Americans" had preceded us. It's an unfortunately common American belief that the most important position is leadership, meaning a domineering and controlling attitude that we all brought with us to a greater or lesser extent. This meant that we often felt it our duty to inform rather than to be informed, to teach rather than learn. This often tainted our relationships with others who weren't from our culture (and sometimes those who were), and diminished in our eyes our own sense of self-worth if we did anything other than speaking or organizing.

When I left Botswana for South Africa I was forced to acknowledge the fact that I felt my role in Botswana to be more important than that in South Africa because it involved giving speeches at schools, where the latter involved the "silent pray-ing" method. But then I learned something from a small inci-dent at Mrs Semela's mother's house that at first I almost allowed to pass unnoticed. When I walked in with my muddy shoes, after the introductions had been made and the tea offered, a little boy no more than six years old was told to clean them. The look on his face when he returned with my shoes, mud-free and brightly polished, wasn't one of annoyance that he'd been asked to perform a menial task, but of pride. Cleaning the guest's shoes was his role that evening, his contribution to hospitality offered by the whole family. The role may have seemed small and insignificant, but was it really? The roles we all play, whether family duties or teaching the Faith, are like the many parts of the same body. A finger may seem small and insignificant, but without it the body is diminished.

Slowly, I grew to feel more satisfied with sitting back and serving as a catalyst, saying prayers in my head for the success of others. This was equally as important as any other role that had to be played in the whole teaching effort. And this, too, was part of being a Bahá'í, a quieter Bahá'í perhaps, but the type of Bahá'í I felt most comfortable being.

Though Hoda's pioneering experiences were home front, in a town across the river from his own that needed a ninth member to form its local Spiritual Assembly, I was delighted to find out how many of his discoveries and realizations mirrored mine – but without the hassle of plane tickets and typhoid shots! I was fortunate to have had the opportunity to serve and travel in foreign lands, but the experience of service to the Cause was not made more significant or acceptable by the purchase of a plane ticket.

I don't know why we grew so close during those few days in Scotland. Even his parents were amazed at how we could sit for hours, talking about places that the other had never been – although it seemed that we had . . . I did know that Hoda's friendship had become too precious a gift to simply leave among journal entries and fading memories. So, when he proposed on our way back to London, I thought about it – for sixteen months – then accepted. But that's another story.

Epilog

I missed the world before I got off the plane; before I walked through the tunnel leading to the airport whose walls I imagined closing in on me, holding me in place and time; before the memories had faded, like bright color does with age, before the sight of my family's faces at the airport – faces of a frozen joy – took me through the first door of my journey.

I wasn't as happy to see them as I thought I'd be, as I dreamt I'd be, ever since my missing them had become a pain in my chest. But I stood hugging them, laughing at their jokes, my smiling face masking my inner thoughts. Inside me a whole ocean sat motionless; motionless and dark and silent.

Everything in the house was just as I remembered it. The same books decorated the same shelves, the same can of pickled artichoke hearts sat in the same cabinet, the same little patches of dirt in the tiled corners of the bathroom. The only thing that had changed was a squeaky hinge in the utensil drawer, that groaned in aggravation when I tried to find a can opener in the middle of the night.

Before Ali went to bed he interrupted a private moment I was having with the open refrigerator, staring into its depths as if it were an audience for one of my stories about Africa. Grabbing the cheese off the shelf he remarked, "As usual, we have nothing to eat." He shot me a few tentative glances as if testing new ground. When I looked at him in amazement he laughed uncomfortably.

"Ali," I said, "I haven't seen this much food in eight months."

But in those eight months I had dined in other ways, and what my stomach had longed for many a night, my spirit had received in plenty.

KEMBA SARAN MAZLOOMIAN

Kemba was born in East Lansing, Michigan in 1971. After graduating from high school in 1989, she served as a Bahá'í youth volunteer for eight months in Botswana, South Africa, Zimbabwe, Mozambique and Namibia. Upon her return to the USA, she enrolled at the University of Michigan. Following her marriage in 1991, she studied English Literature for a year at the Universities of Sussex and Middlesex in England. She graduated in 1995 with a Bachelor of Arts Degree in English, and a Bachelor of Science degree in Architecture. Kemba lives with her husband in Ann Arbor, where she is currently studying for a Master's degree. *To Dine with the Blameless Ethiopians* is her first book.